FOR THE LIFE OF THE WORLD

Toward a Social Ethos of the Orthodox Church

Cover art and design by Paul Y. Loboda; illustrations by Predrag Ilievski;
Cover art and illustrations copyright © Newrome Press.

Publisher's Cataloging-In-Publication Data

Names: Hart, David Bentley, 1956- editor. | Chryssavgis, John, editor.
Title: For the life of the world : toward a social ethos of the Orthodox
Church / edited by David Bentley Hart and John Chryssavgis.
Description: Brookline [Massachusetts] : Holy Cross Orthodox Press,
2020. | Includes bibliographical references and index.
Identifiers: ISBN 9781935317807
Subjects: LCSH: Orthodox Eastern Church--Doctrines. | Social problems-
-Religious aspects--Orthodox Eastern Church. | Social ethics.
Classification: LCC BX320.3 .S73 2020 | DDC 230/.19--dc23

FOR THE LIFE
OF THE WORLD

Toward a Social Ethos of the Orthodox Church

Edited by David Bentley Hart and John Chryssavgis

HOLY CROSS
ORTHODOX PRESS

BROOKLINE
2020

CONTENTS

TRANSLATION
Protocol No. 840/2019

To the very reverend John Chryssavgis, Archdeacon of the Ecumenical Throne, our beloved son in the Lord: may God's grace and peace be with you.

Having formally evaluated in session of the Holy and Sacred Synod the draft document "For the Life of the World: Toward a Social Ethos of the Orthodox Church," created with your initiative, proposal and participation by a group of theologians specifically charged with this task, in the spirit and context of the decisions of the Holy and Great Council convened in Crete, with a view to developing, cultivating and disseminating its teaching, through this Patriarchal Letter and by Synodal Decree, we hereby express to you and all members of this editorial and scholarly Commission that labored so selflessly our commendation and congratulations as well as our wholehearted gratitude for this extraordinary response and the submission of this exceptional essay.

Therefore, upon favorably assessing this comprehensive document, which provides the parameters and guidelines for the social responsibility of our Church before the complex challenges and problems of today's world, without at the same time overlooking the favorable potential and positive perspectives of contemporary civilization, the Holy and Sacred Synod of the Ecumenical Patriarchate approves its formal publication as the fruit of a collective theological achievement.

Wherefore, through our Patriarchal blessing, we invest upon you and all those who worked tirelessly for the fulfilment of this profound task the grace and illumination of the All-Holy Spirit of wisdom and prudence.

At the Phanar, on January 18, 2020

Your fervent supplicant before God

† BARTHOLOMEW

Archbishop of Constantinople-New Rome
and Ecumenical Patriarch

Ἀριθμ. Πρωτ. 840/2019

Τῷ Ἱερολογιωτάτῳ Ἀρχιδιακόνῳ τοῦ Οἰκουμενικοῦ Θρόνου κυρίῳ Ἰωάννῃ Χρυσαυγῆ, τέκνῳ τῆς ἡμῶν Μετριότητος ἐν Κυρίῳ ἀγαπητῷ, χάριν καὶ εἰρήνην παρὰ Θεοῦ.

Κατόπιν θεωρήσεως ἐν συνεδρίᾳ τῆς περὶ ἡμᾶς Ἁγίας καὶ Ἱερᾶς Συνόδου τοῦ ἐν σχεδίῳ Κειμένου «Ἵνα ζωὴν ἔχωσιν, καὶ περισσὸν ἔχωσιν. Τὸ κοινωνικὸν ἦθος ἐν τῇ Ὀρθοδόξῳ Ἐκκλησίᾳ», καταρτισθέντος, ὑμετέρᾳ πρωτοβουλίᾳ, προτάσει καὶ συμμετοχῇ, ὑπὸ ὁμάδος εἰδικῶς πρὸς τοῦτο ἐξονομασθέντων Θεολόγων, ἐν τῷ πνεύματι καὶ κατὰ τὰς ἀποφάσεις τῆς ἐν Κρήτῃ συνελθούσης Ἁγίας καὶ Μεγάλης Συνόδου, πρὸς ἀνάπτυξιν, καλλιέργειαν καὶ διάδοσιν τῆς σχετικῆς διδασκαλίας αὐτῆς, προαγόμεθα, ἀποφάσει συνοδικῇ, ἵνα ἐκφράσωμεν διὰ τοῦ παρόντος Πατριαρχικοῦ ἡμῶν Γράμματος τῇ ὑμετέρᾳ ἀγαπητῇ Ἱερολογιότητι καὶ πᾶσι τοῖς θυσιαστικῶς κοπιάσασι μέλεσι τῆς ἐν λόγῳ Συντακτικῆς Ἐπιστημονικῆς Ἐπιτροπῆς, τὴν εὐαρέσκειαν, τὰ συγχαρητήρια καὶ τὰς ὁλοθύμους εὐχαριστίας ἡμῶν ἐπὶ τῇ πρόφρονι ἀνταποκρίσει καὶ τῇ ὑποβολῇ τῆς περισπουδάστου ταύτῃ μελέτης.

Ἡ Ἁγία καὶ Ἱερὰ Σύνοδος τοῦ Οἰκουμενικοῦ Πατριαρχείου, ἀξιολογήσασα τὸ μεστὸν τοῦτο κείμενον, τὸ ὁποῖον θεματοποιεῖ τοὺς ὅρους καὶ τὰς διαστάσεις τῆς κοινωνικῆς ἀποστολῆς τῆς Ἐκκλησίας ἐνώπιον τῶν προκλήσεων, τῶν προβλημάτων καὶ τῶν ἀδιεξόδων τοῦ συγχρόνου κόσμου, χωρὶς νὰ ἀγνοῇ τὰς θετικὰς δυνατότητας καὶ προοπτικὰς τοῦ πολιτισμοῦ του, ἐγκρίνει τὴν τύποις ἔκδοσιν αὐτοῦ ὡς καρποῦ συλλογικῆς θεολογικῆς ἐργασίας.

Ἐπὶ δὲ τούτοις, καταστέφοντες ὑμᾶς διὰ τῆς Πατριαρχικῆς ἡμῶν εὐλογίας, ἐπικαλούμεθα ἐπὶ τὴν ὑμετέραν Ἱερολογιότητα καὶ ἐπὶ πάντας τοὺς φιλοτίμως ἐργασθέντας διὰ τὴν ὁλοκλήρωσιν τοῦ ἐμβριθοῦς τούτου πονήματος, τὴν χάριν καὶ τὸν φωτισμὸν τοῦ Παναγίου Πνεύματος τῆς σοφίας καὶ τῆς συνέσεως.

βκ΄ Ἰανουαρίου ιη΄

FOREWORD

This is my commandment:
that you love one another, as I have loved you. (John 15:12)

The appearance of this needful and excellent text, "For the Life of the World: Toward a Social Ethos of the Orthodox Church," presents a mature and reasoned discourse about our engagement with the world and with each other, not only to the Orthodox Christian Faithful, but to all people of good will. Let us be grateful to the First Throne of Orthodoxy, the Ecumenical Patriarchate of Constantinople, for Her patronage of its contributors and editors, and her sanction of its substance. Just as a good mother teaches her children well, the Holy Mother and Great Church of Christ offers these considerations for the edification and enrichment of all, under the exceptional leadership of His All-Holiness Ecumenical Patriarch Bartholomew, whose depth of vision and breadth of experience lend invaluable perspective to the apostolate of the Church.

This statement does not pronounce clear-cut responses to social challenges, but instead proposes general guidelines to difficult questions. Like every published document, the work may convey a sense of something finished and complete, but it is actually an initiation of a continuing conversation, an ongoing meditation on what "the Spirit is saying to the Churches" (Revelation 2:7). As Orthodox Christians, we know that the Lord Jesus Christ said and did so much more than is recorded, such that if everything had been written down, the world itself could not contain the books (cf. John 21:19). Therefore, as his disciples of our own day and time, we are responsible to bring forth the manifestation of the "great love with which he loved us" (Ephesians 2:4), from his divine teaching and the unbroken and uncompromised tradition of his apostles and disciples throughout history.

In a very real sense, what follows in these pages is a continuation of the sacred and profound work of the historic Holy and Great Council of Crete (2016). This ongoing extrapolation of the Council's pastoral and ministerial accomplishment is a practical and pastoral, rather than an academic or analytical, application of the essential teachings of the Christian Faith. Each heading defines an area of Christian concern, presenting theological context and spiritual perspectives in a clearly elucidated discourse. The text is most apt for furthering conversations about current and open-ended questions of contemporary life.

In the end, what this text does is open us up to the implications of what it means to be loved by God, and to respond to that love by loving one another. It speaks to the best of our shared humanity, acknowledging from its first paragraph that every human being is created to "look up to and see God," even as the very word "human" in Greek, "ἄνθρωπος" derives from "ἄνω θρώσκειν," to "leap up on high."

Indeed, we are created and destined to live in such a way that we reflect the love of our Creator for every creature. This text offers to the reader, who is willing to listen, insight and guidance on how to participate in life in the world, all the while enjoying the life in the Spirit. It is my prayer and hope that its enlightened discourse will spur all of us to lift our sights to our higher purpose, to the better angels of our nature, and to richer and deeper communion with God and with one another.

HOLY PASCHA 2020

† ELPIDOPHOROS

Archbishop of America

PREFACE

The Origin of this Document

In June 2017, His All-Holiness Ecumenical Patriarch Bartholomew appointed a special commission of theologians

> to prepare a formal document on the social doctrine of the Orthodox Church, as this has been reflected and expressed in the tradition through the centuries and by the Ecumenical Patriarchate in contemporary practice, particularly as recently adopted in the documents and decisions of the Holy and Great Council held in Crete in June 2016.

The mandate of the special commission was

> to submit a text in timely manner for consideration and approval by the Holy and Sacred Synod of the Church of Constantinople. The fruit of this deliberation and composition will subsequently be published for the benefit of our faithful throughout the world in order to serve as a solid foundation for reference and conversation on vital issues and challenges facing the world today.

In December 2017, the Ecumenical Patriarch issued a formal encyclical to the Hierarchs of the Throne, who have assumed the burden of pastoral service to the spiritual children of the Ecumenical Patriarchate and who experience the present issues and enormous challenges first-hand, thereby acquiring a pastoral experience that is most precious for the entire Body of the Church for the purpose of addressing these matters,

requesting that each provide suggestions "concerning the nature of the signs of our times as well as ways of responding to these challenges in the spirit of the Orthodox spiritual and pastoral tradition" and encouraging each of them "to submit a report on the urgent social problems" faced by the faithful today, as well as "a pastoral response in the context of an Orthodox ecclesiastical witness in the modern world." Over the next two months, more than twenty-five eparchies of the Ecumenical Throne responded in detail, many of them inviting clergymen and theologians, specialists and scholars, as well as social workers and civil leaders to contribute to an informed report.

After formal submission to the Holy and Sacred Synod in September 2019, the commission document was referred for assessment to Hierarchs of the Synod and Hierarchs of the Eparchies in October 2019. In January 2020, the Holy and Sacred Synod of the Ecumenical Patriarchate

favorably evaluated this comprehensive document, formally expressing its commendation and congratulations as well as its wholehearted gratitude for the extraordinary response and exceptional work of the commission, while approving the statement for publication by the members of the commission in order to provide parameters and guidelines for the social responsibility of the Orthodox Church before the challenges and perspectives of today's world, without at the same time overlooking the favorable potential and perspectives of contemporary civilization.

The Theological Background

The task of producing a single statement of the social doctrine of the Orthodox Church is of its nature a complicated, not to say contentious, undertaking. The Orthodox Church operates within a vast variety of cultural and historical contexts, each with its own social and political concerns and traditions. The Church regards its social teaching as nothing other than a faithful transcription of the moral teachings of the gospel into the language of public ethics and policy, and insists that every Orthodox Christian is called to live in the world as a faithful disciple of Christ, called to fellowship with the whole communion of saints. That said, the process of translating the commands of Christ into the principles of social life is always a delicate matter, often ambiguous, and rarely easy; thus any reflection on Orthodox social doctrine must rely upon the accumulated experience and wisdom of the Church as a whole, throughout the world and throughout her history. Orthodox tradition has continuously grown and been enriched in the course of its journey through the centuries, and from that long experience the Church ceaselessly draws guidance—signposts along the way, so to speak—in reflecting upon social and ethical issues. As Fr. Georges Florovsky observed: "The Church gives us not a system, but a key; not a plan of God's city, but the means of entering it."[1]

In our time, the Church frequently finds itself ill-prepared to respond to the realities of pluralism and globalization, or for that matter of individualism and secularization. In many societies, the Church is tempted simply to stand in opposition to the world, often sweepingly denouncing and despising all its forms and fashions. All too often, those who presume to speak for Orthodox tradition believe that the Church can preserve her integrity only by turning blindly away from the present and uncritically toward the past, seeking shelter in a petrified and sentimentalized vision of the Christian orders of earlier centuries. Holy tradition, however, is much more than a static deposit inherited from the past, requiring nothing more than assiduous curatorship and rote repetition. It is not simply a memorial to the words of the Fathers of old, but is rather the living and dynamic reality to which those words pointed, the ever abiding presence of the Holy Spirit who descended on the Apostles at Pentecost, a constant and ever-new pilgrimage toward the Kingdom that is to come. It is this living tradition that inspires the Church to recover its sacred calling and that endows her with the divine courage to transform the world with all its new challenges from within,

> to offer witness not so much from a polemical perspective, but from that of an 'incarnational' mission, following the example of the incarnate Word by speaking to the contemporary world 'from within'—

---

1   Georges Florovsky, "The Catholicity of the Church, in *Bible, Church, Tradition: An Eastern Orthodox View*, Collected Works, vol. 1, Belmont, MA: Nordland, 1972, 50.

bearing its crosses and striving to understand its anguish.[2]

The Orthodox Church has long nurtured within herself a strong and distinctive social instinct, one that has often risen to the surface when historical circumstances have been propitious, and that even now constitutes her principal contribution to modern discussions of social ethics. Metropolitan Kallistos draws a clear connection between this social conscience and the doctrine of the Holy Trinity:

> Our belief in a Trinitarian God, in a God of social inter-relationship and shared love, commits us to opposing all forms of exploitation, injustice, and discrimination. In our struggle for human rights, we are acting in the name of the Trinity.[3]

And Mother Maria Skobtsova (St. Maria of Paris) sees the Church's social vision as emanating from the sacrament of the Eucharist:

> If at the center the Church's life there is this sacrificial, self-giving Eucharistic love, then where are the Church's boundaries, where is the periphery of this center? Here it is possible to speak of the whole of Christianity as an eternal offering of the divine liturgy beyond church walls . . . and the whole world becomes the one altar of a single temple.[4]

2   Metropolitan John [Zizioulas] of Pergamon, in *Person, Eucharist, and Kingdom of Heaven: Orthodox and Ecumenical Perspectives. Essays in Honor of Metropolitan John [Zizioulas] of Pergamon*, eds Pantelis Kalaitzidis and Nikolaos Asproulis, Volos: Dimitrias Editions, 2016, 332 [In Greek].

3   Metropolitan Kallistos Ware, "The human person as icon of the Trinity," *Sobornost*, 8.2, 1986, 6–23 at 18.

4   Maria Skobtsova, "Types of Religious Life," *Mother Maria Skobtsova: Essential Writings*, Maryknoll, New York: Orbis Books, 2002, 185.

The Pastoral Dimensions

In attempting to articulate Orthodox social doctrine in terms appropriate to modern realities—which was inevitably a somewhat monumental task—the commission strove to remain mindful of certain fundamental concerns specifically identified by His All-Holiness Ecumenical Patriarch Bartholomew, as well as of others identified by those Hierarchs of the Ecumenical Throne around the world who took the time to communicate their most urgent pastoral concerns. These guidelines served as general parameters, not as rigid boundaries, but they provided the commission inestimable aid in discharging its extraordinary responsibility. In adhering to those guidelines, moreover, the commission tried to avoid nebulous abstractions and sweeping generalizations, preferring to offer specific principles for consideration and adoption by the faithful and their communities. In regard to every topic addressed, the commission sought to remain faithful to the historical teachings of the Church, even in attempting to bring those teachings into direct engagement with modern concerns. It endeavored to steer well clear of simplistic, pietistic, or legalistic pronouncements, but it sought no less sedulously to avoid presenting the personal opinions of its members as authoritative statements of Orthodox teaching. No claim is advanced in these pages that was not arrived at through a scrupulous contemplation of the biblical, patristic, dogmatic, and theological sources of the tradition as a whole. Finally, conscious of the constant struggle of all Christians to live faithful lives in a frequently unsettled and uncharitable world, the commission sought to abstain altogether from the language and intonations of judgment or condemnation.

The document aspires to reflect the worldview and mission of the Ecumenical Patriarchate, as expressed both down the centuries, up to the present day. Though the structure and style of this text are rather formal, the commission strove to avoid empty abstraction and to offer concrete moral proposals. The document's intentions are purely pastoral, moreover; its analysis of the present is meant to be compassionate, its critiques strictly constructive, and its exhortations studiously humble. If it fails in any of these respects, the commission takes full responsibility for the deficiency. It was undertaken, moreover, with a genuine willingness to learn not only from the wisdom of earlier generations, but also from the mistakes, as well as to learn from one another in the communion of the Church. In this regard, the members of the commission submit this service to the church at large as a preliminary step toward a far more expansive theological dialogue and as an aid to spiritual growth for the Orthodox faithful.

David Bentley Hart   John Chryssavgis

Members of the Commission:

Rev. Dr. John Chryssavgis,
Ecumenical Patriarchate (chair)

Dr. David Bentley Hart,
Notre Dame University Institute for Advanced Study

Dr. George Demacopoulos,
Fordham University

Dr. Carrie Frederick Frost,
St. Sophia Ukrainian Orthodox Seminary

Rev. Dr. Brandon Gallaher,
University of Exeter

Rev. Dr. Perry Hamalis,
North Central College

Rev. Dr. Nicolas Kazarian,
Greek Orthodox Archdiocese of America

Dr. Aristotle Papanikolaou,
Fordham University

Dr. James Skedros,
Holy Cross School of Theology

Dr. Gayle Woloschak,
Northwestern University

Dr. Konstantinos Delikostantis,
Ecumenical Patriarchate

Dr. Theodoros Yiangou,
University of Thessaloniki

Secretary

Nicholas Anton,
Greek Orthodox Archdiocese of America

Acknowledgements:

It was a profound honor to be appointed members of this special commission and a distinctive privilege to be assigned this mandate by His All-Holiness Ecumenical Patriarch Bartholomew. The members of the commission express their thanks for his confidence, auspices, and endorsement.

His Eminence Archbishop Elpidophoros of America was generously and graciously supportive of the publication of this statement online, in translation, and in print.

We are grateful for the invaluable insights of Elder Metropolitan John of Pergamon (Ecumenical Patriarchate) and Metropolitan Kallistos of Diokleia (University of Oxford).

Moreover, we recognize the support of Metropolitans Savas of Pittsburgh, Evangelos of New Jersey, and Nathanael of Chicago. Metropolitan Methodios of Boston and the Department of Inter-Orthodox, Ecumenical, and Interfaith Relations of the Greek Orthodox Archdiocese of America (through a grant of Leadership 100) sponsored the translation of the document into several languages.

Finally, we thank Holy Cross Orthodox Press for the elegant production and George M. Cantonis, President of Hellenic College and Holy Cross School of Theology, for the propitious publication of this book in light of the official visit of His All-Holiness Ecumenical Patriarch Bartholomew to the United States in May 2020.

FOR THE LIFE OF THE WORLD

Toward a Social Ethos of the Orthodox Church

I. INTRODUCTION

It is time to serve the Lord

§1 The Orthodox Church understands the human person as having been created in the image and likeness of God. To be made in God's image is to be made for free and conscious communion and union with God in Jesus Christ, inasmuch as we are formed in, through, and for him. St. Basil the Great tells us that, of all animals, the human being was created upright so that it might look up to and see God, worshipping him and acknowledging Him as his source and origin. Instead of "being dragged down to earth . . . his head is lifted high toward things above, that he may look up to what is akin to him."[1] And as we are made to be in communion with God in Jesus Christ, Irenaeus of Lyons writes that the human being was made in "image of Christ."[2] This service

Genesis 1:26

Colossians 1:16

2 Corinthians 4:4

---

1 Basil of Caesarea, Discourse 2, 15: On the Origin of Humanity, in *On the Human Condition*, Crestwood, NY: St Vladimir's Seminary Press, 61.

2 Irenaeus of Lyons, *On the Apostolic Preaching*, Crestwood, NY: St Vladimir's Seminary Press, 1997, 22.

through prayer and action is derived from loving praise and reverent gratitude for life and for all the gifts that God imparts through his Son and in his Spirit. Our service to God is fundamentally doxological in nature and essentially Eucharist in character.

§2   To say we are made to serve God is to say we are made for loving communion: communion with the Kingdom of the Father and of the Son and of the Holy Spirit; and through communion with God as Trinity, human beings are also called into loving communion with their neighbors and the whole cosmos. Our actions are to flow from love of God and loving union with him in and through Christ, in whom we meet and treat our brother and sister as our very life.[3] This communion with Christ in the face of our neighbor is what lies behind the first and great commandment of the Law to love God with one's whole heart and one's neighbor as oneself.[4]

Matthew 22:37–39

§3   Being made in the image and likeness of God, each person is unique and infinitely precious, and each is a special object of God's love. As Christ taught, *even the hairs of [y]our head are all numbered.* The immensity and particularity of God's love for each of us, and for all of creation, surpasses human understanding. It is imparted to us with an absolute generosity, by a God mindful not of our sins but of his own will that none should perish, but rather that all should be saved and come to know the truth. Hence it is a love that seeks to form each of us into ever greater conformity with God's own goodness, and that therefore

Luke 12:7

2 Peter 3:9

1 Timothy 2:4

---

3   *Sayings of the Desert Fathers*, Anthony the Great, 9, 3. PG 65.77B.

4   See Basil, *Ethics* 3–5. See *On Christian Ethics*, Yonkers, NY: St. Vladimir's Seminary Press, 2015.

tirelessly enjoins us to seek to cultivate in ourselves—in
thought, word, and deed—a love for our neighbor, and
for all our fellow creatures, as unstinting as God's own. It   *Matthew 5:43–48*
calls us to an ever greater communion with one another,
with all those whose lives we touch, with the fullness of
creation, and thus with him who is the creator of all. The
ultimate destiny, moreover, to which we are summoned,
is nothing less than our *theosis*: our deification and transformation by the Holy Spirit into members of the body
of Christ, joined in the Son to the Father, whereby we become true partakers of the divine nature. In the words of
St. Athanasius: "The Son of God became human so that
we might become divine."[5] But, then, this must be a corporate destiny, as it is only through our participation in
the community of Christ's body that any of us, as a unique
object of divine love, can enter into full union with God.
Our spiritual lives, therefore, cannot fail also to be social
lives. Our piety cannot fail also to be an ethos.

$4   The world we inhabit is a fallen order, broken and dark-
ened, enslaved to death and sin, tormented by violence
and injustice. Such is not the condition God wishes for
his creation; it is the consequence of an ancient estrange-
ment of our world from its maker. As such, it is a reality that can in no way dictate or determine the limits of
our moral responsibilities to our fellow creatures. We
are called to serve a Kingdom not of this world, in ser-   *John 18:36*
vice to a peace that this world cannot give. We are called,   *John 14:27*
therefore, not to accommodate ourselves to the practical
exigencies of the world as we find it, but instead ever and

---

5   Athanasius, *On the Incarnation* 54.3. PG 25b.192B. See *Athanasius:* Contra
Gentes *and* De Incarnatione, Oxford, UK: Oxford University Press, 1971, 268.

again to strive against evil, however invincible it may at times appear, and to work for the love and justice that God requires of his creatures, however impractical that may at times prove. On the path to communion with God, it is humanity's vocation not merely to accept—but rather to bless, elevate, and *transfigure*—this world, so that its intrinsic goodness may be revealed even amidst its fallenness. This is the special purpose of human life, the high priestly calling of creatures endowed with rational freedom and conscience. We know, of course, that this work of transfiguration will never be complete in this life, and can reach its fulfillment only in the Kingdom of God; still, however, our works of love bear fruit in this life, and they are required of all who would enter the life of the age to *Matthew 25:31–46* come. The Church knows that such efforts are never in vain, moreover, because the Holy Spirit is also at work in all the labors of the faithful, bringing all thing to their fru- *Romans 8:28* ition in due season.

§5   As the requirements of Christian love are unremitting, those who are joined to Christ may on many occasions be called to pursue God's goodness even to the point of self-sacrifice, after the model of their Lord. The work of transfiguring the cosmos is also a struggle against everything distorted and malignant, both in ourselves and in the damaged structure and fabric of a suffering creation; and this means that, inevitably, this work must be an ascetical labor. To a very great degree, we are called to strive against the obstinate selfishness of our own sinful inclinations, and to undertake a constant effort to cultivate in ourselves the eye of charity, which alone is able to see the face of Christ in the face of our every brother and sister, "the least of these," whom we meet as though each of them were Christ himself. Hence the Apostle Paul's use of the image of the athlete in training as a metaphor for the Christian life. But this labor should also be undertaken in common, as the corporate effort of a single body whose many members sustain and support one another in a life of shared love and service. This is truly a work of love, not of fear. It is the natural expression of a life transformed by the Holy Spirit, a life of joy, at whose communal heart stands the Eucharist, the ever-renewed celebration of God's lavish self-donation, the sharing of his very flesh and blood for the life of the world. In giving himself always anew in the Eucharistic mystery, Christ draws us forever to himself, and thereby draws us to one another. He also grants us a foretaste of that wedding-feast of the Kingdom to which all persons are called, even those who are at present outside the visible communion of the Church. However great the labors of Christians in this world, out of obedience to the law of divine love, they are sustained by a deeper and ultimately irrepressible rejoicing.

Matthew 25:40, 45

1 Corinthians 9:24–27

§6   The surest warrant for and charter of an Orthodox social ethos is found, before all else, in the teachings of Christ. No feature of our Lord's Gospel is more pronounced and constant than his absolute concern and compassion for the poor and disenfranchised, the abused and neglected, the imprisoned, the hungry, the weary and heavy-laden, the despairing. His condemnations of the luxuriance of the wealthy, of indifference to the plight of the oppressed, and of exploitation of the destitute are uncompromising and unequivocal. At the same time, the tenderness of his love for "the least of these" is boundless. No one who aspires to be a follower of Christ can fail to imitate either his indignation at injustice or his love for the oppressed. In this regard, Christ's teachings confirm, while making even more urgent, the largest and most universal moral demands made by the Law and the Prophets of Israel: provision for the destitute, care for the stranger, justice for the wronged, mercy for all. We find the most resplendent examples of Christian social morality, in fact, in the life of the Apostolic Church, which in an age of empire created for itself a new kind of polity, set apart from the hierarchies of human governance and all the social and political violences, chronic and acute, upon which those hierarchies subsist. The earliest Christians were a community committed to a radical life of love, in which all other allegiances—nation, race, class—were replaced by a singular fidelity to Christ's law of charity. It was a community established in the knowledge that in Christ there is neither Jew nor Greek, neither slave nor free, nor any division in dignity between man and woman, because all *Galatians 3:28* are one. And so, also, it was a community that shared all things in common, that provided for those in need, that permitted those with means to return to the common *Acts 2:42–46; 4:32–35* good the bounty they had reaped from creation, and that required no laws and no powers of enforcement except those of love. Though the Orthodox Church knows that society as a whole operates upon different principles than these, and that Christians have it in their power to remedy social ills to only a limited degree at any time and in any place, still it holds up the ideal of the Apostolic Church as the purest expression of Christian charity as a social logic and communal practice, and judges all human political and social arrangements in light of that divinely ordained model.

§7   All peoples possess some knowledge of the good, and all are able to some degree to perceive the requirements of justice and mercy. Though the children of Israel were especially blessed in receiving the Law of Moses, and though the Church enjoys a special knowledge of the love of God as revealed in the person of Christ, still the deepest moral commandments of God's law are inscribed upon every human heart, and speak to the human intellect and *Romans 2:15* will as the promptings of conscience. Thus, as Irenaeus says, the divine precepts necessary for salvation are implanted in humankind from the beginning of time;[6] and these laws, "which are natural, and noble, and common to all" were then amplified and enriched and deepened in the new covenant of liberty imparted by Christ to his Church.[7] These precepts are "the law of the mind";[8] they are among the deepest rational principles, the eternal *logoi*, written upon the foundation of creation and residing eternally in the *Logos*, the divine Son.[9] Hence, in many cases, "conscience and reason suffice in the Law's stead."[10]

6   Irenaeus, *Against the Heresies* 4.15.1. See Sources Chrétiennes 100, Paris: Cerf, 1965, 548–549.

7   Irenaeus, *Against the Heresies*, 4.16.5. See Sources Chrétiennes 100, Paris: Cerf, 1965 571–572.

8   John of Damascus, *The Orthodox Faith*, 4.22. PG 94.1200B. See *St. John of Damascus: Writings*, The Fathers of the Church 37, Washington, DC: Catholic University of America Press, 1958, 389.

9   Maximus the Confessor, *Ambiguum* 42. PG91.1329C. See *On Difficulties in the Church Fathers*, Dumbarton Oaks Medieval Library 28, Cambridge, MA: Harvard University Press, 2014, vol. 2, 123–187.

10   John Chrysostom, *Epistle to the Romans*, Homily 5.5. PG 60.429.

But in Christ we have received a new outpouring of the Spirit and have become a new holy priestly people, under this new covenant of liberty—a covenant that does not abolish the natural law, but rather enlarges its range and makes its demands upon us absolute. This means that Christians are permitted, and in fact obliged, to act as a prophetic presence in the world, speaking not only to the closed company of the baptized but to the whole of creation, recalling human beings everywhere to the decrees written into their very nature, and summoning them to the sanctifying labor of justice and mercy. And we take the Mother of God as our great exemplar here, for it is she, in her freely given assent to become the place of the advent of divine love in person—in her cooperation *(synergeia)* with God—who has bequeathed to us the purest model of true obedience to God's law: a willingness to give ourselves entirely to the presence of God's Son, to become the shelter and tabernacle of his indwelling in this world, to receive God's *Logos* as at once the highest vocation and the greatest fulfillment of our nature.

II. THE CHURCH IN THE PUBLIC SPHERE

Let us commend our whole life unto Christ our God

§8 Christian hope lies in the Kingdom of God and not in the kingdoms of this world. The Church puts her *trust not in princes, in sons of men, in whom there is no salvation,* but rather in the Son of God who has entered history to liberate his creatures from all those practices and structures of sin, oppression, and violence that corrupt the fallen world. Over the course of Christian history, Christians have lived

*Psalm 146[145]:3
References to the
Septuagint are in
[brackets].*

under diverse forms of government—empires, totalitarian regimes, liberal democracies, nations with Christian establishments, nations with other established creeds, secular states—some of which have proved amicable to the institutional Church, some hostile, and some indifferent. No matter what the political regime to which they have been subject, however, the principal home of Christians in this world is in the celebration (at times open, at times in secret) of the holy Eucharist, where they are enjoined to "set aside all earthly care" (Divine Liturgy of St. John Chrysostom) and to enter at once both into the unity of the body of Christ in history and into the joy of God's Kingdom beyond history. The Eucharist, in being celebrated and shared by the faithful, ever and again constitutes the true Christian polity, and shines out as an icon of God's Kingdom as it will be realized in a redeemed, transfigured, and glorified creation. As such, the Eucharist is a prophetic sign as well, at once a critique of all political regimes insofar as they fall short of divine love and an invitation to all peoples to *seek first the Kingdom of God and its justice. Here we have no enduring city, and must look instead for the city that is to come; here we are strangers and pilgrims*; but here also we enjoy a foretaste of that final redemption of all social order in God's Kingdom, and have been entrusted with a sign to exhibit before the nations, by which to call them to a life of peace and charity under the shelter of God's promises.

Matthew 6:33

Hebrews 13:14

Hebrews 11:13

§9 The Orthodox Church cannot judge all forms of human government as equivalent with one another, even though all fall far short of the Kingdom. It unequivocally condemns every kind of institutional corruption and totalitarianism, for instance, knowing that it can bring nothing but mass suffering and oppression. Neither does the Church insist that Christian citizens of established states are required in every conceivable situation to submit to the powers that be or to consent to the social and political orders in which they find themselves. Of course, Christ himself acknowledged the right of the civil authority to collect taxes when he said, *render therefore to Caesar* *Matthew 22:21* *the things that are Caesar's*. And it is true that, in very special circumstances, the Apostle Paul enjoined the Christians in Rome to obey the justly constituted civil authority of the city and empire, and even recognized the legitimate authority of those who "carry the short-sword"—*machai-rophoroi*, which is to say soldiers, military policemen, civil guards, or taxation enforcement officers—empowered to *Romans 13:1–7* preserve civic peace. But this isolated counsel clearly does not constitute any kind of absolute rule for Christian conduct in all imaginable circumstances. This we know from the words of the Apostle Peter to the Council in Jerusalem, which was the duly appointed legal authority of Judaea: When the commands of even a legally established political authority contradict our responsibilities as Christians, *we* *Acts 5:29* *must obey God rather than men*. More to the point, Paul's admonitions to the Christians of Rome concerned only the situation of the Church under a pagan imperial authority, and tell us nothing now regarding how Christians should seek to order society and promote civic peace when they themselves wield power, or regarding what Christians may require of peoples and governments when exercising their prophetic vocation to proclaim and witness to God's justice and mercy to the world. Even Christ, in cleansing the Jerusalem Temple of moneychangers and merchants, did not hesitate to defy both the policing powers of the Judean Temple authorities and Rome's universal ordinances against civic disorders. The Church should, of course, seek to live at peace with all persons in whatever lands it inhabits, and to offer that peace to everyone; and in most cases this requires obedience to the laws that exist in those lands. Even so, the Church remains in some sense always an alien presence within any human order, and recognizes that God's judgment falls upon all human political power in some measure. Christians may and often must participate in the political life of the societies in which they live, but must do so always in service to the justice and mercy of God's Kingdom. Such was the injunction from the earliest Christian period: "We have been taught to pay all proper respect to powers and authorities of God's appointment, so long as it does not compromise us."[11] At times, this may entail participation not by way of perfect obedience, but by way of the higher citizenship of civil disobedience, even rebellion. The Kingdom of God alone is the Christian's first and last loyalty, and all other allegiances are at most provisional, transient, partial, and incidental.

§10   In many countries in the world today, civil order, freedom, human rights, and democracy are realities in which citizens may trust; and, to a very real degree, these societies accord persons the fundamental dignity of the liberty to seek and pursue the good ends they desire for themselves, their families, and their communities. This is a very rare blessing indeed, viewed in relation to the

---

11   *The Martyrdom of Polycarp*, 10. PG 5.1037A. *Early Christian Writers: The Apostolic Fathers*, New York, NY: Penguin Books, 1987 [revised], 128.

entire course of human history, and it would be irrational
and uncharitable of Christians not to feel a genuine gratitude for the special democratic genius of the modern age.
Orthodox Christians who enjoy the great advantages of
living in such countries should not take such values for
granted, but should instead actively support them, and
work for the preservation and extension of democratic
institutions and customs within the legal, cultural, and
economic frameworks of their respective societies. It is
something of a dangerous temptation among Orthodox
Christians to surrender to a debilitating and in many
respects fantastical nostalgia for some long-vanished
golden era, and to imagine that it constituted something
like the sole ideal Orthodox polity. This can become an especially pernicious kind of false piety, one that mistakes
the transient political forms of the Orthodox past, such
as the Byzantine Empire, for the essence of the Church
of the Apostles. The special advantages of the Church
under Christian rule may have allowed for the gestation
and formation of a distinct Orthodox ethos within the political spaces inhabited by Orthodox Christians, but they
also had the unfortunate additional effect of binding the
Church to certain crippling limitations. Far too often, the
Orthodox Church has allowed for the conflation of national, ethnic, and religious identity, to the point that the
external forms and language of the faith—quite evacu-
ated of their true content—have come to be used as instruments for advancing national and cultural interests
under the guise of Christian adherence. And this has often inhibited the Church in its vocation to proclaim the
Gospel to all peoples.

$11   Thus it was that the Council of Constantinople in 1872 condemned "phyletism," which is to say the subordination of the Orthodox faith to ethnic identities and national interests. A love for one's own culture is an honorable sentiment, so long as it is a generous sentiment as well, allied to a willingness to recognize the beauty and nobility of other cultures, and to welcome exchanges between and fruitful intermixtures of all cultures. And patriotism can be a benign and wholesome feeling, so long as it is not mistaken for a virtue in itself, or for a moral good even when one's country has become profoundly unjust or destructive. But it is absolutely forbidden for Christians to make an idol of cultural, ethnic, or national identity. There can be no such thing as a "Christian nationalism," or even any form of nationalism tolerable to Christian conscience. This must, unfortunately, be emphasized at the present moment, on account of the unexpected recrudescence in much of the developed world of the most insidious ideologies of identity, including belligerent forms of nationalism and blasphemous philosophies of race. The crimes born of racial injustice—from the early modern rebirth of chattel slavery along racial lines to the later regimes of South African apartheid or legal segregation in the United States, all of which were enforced by violence both organized and random—are very much a part of the whole of modern Western history, of course; but racialist ideology as such is a toxic relic of the superstitions of the pseudo-science of the late eighteenth to early twentieth centuries. And, while genuine scientific advances (in such areas as molecular v, genomics especially) have exposed the very concept of distinct races—or of separate genetic clades within the human species—as a vicious fantasy, with no basis in biological reality, the poisonous notion of race remains a part of the conceptual world of late modernity. There could be no greater contradiction of the Gospel. There is only one human race, to which all persons belong, and all are called as one to become a single people in God the creator. There is no humanity apart from the one universal humanity that the Son of God assumed in becoming human, and it embraces all persons without distinction or discrimination. And yet, sadly, the rise of new forms of political and nationalist extremism has even resulted in the infiltration of various Orthodox communities by individuals committed to race-theory. The Orthodox Church condemns their views without qualification, and calls them to a complete repentance and penitential reconciliation with the body of Christ. And it must be incumbent on every Orthodox community, when it discovers such persons in its midst and cannot move them to renounce the evils they promote, to expose, denounce, and expel them. Any ecclesial community that fails in this has betrayed Christ.

§12   No matter what the political arrangements in which Orthodox Christians find themselves, when they emerge from their celebration of the holy Eucharist they must reenter the world always anew as witnesses to God's eternal Kingdom. In their encounters with others who do not share their faith, Orthodox Christians must remember that all human beings are living and irreplaceable icons of God, fashioned for him in their inmost nature. No one should seek to advance the Christian faith through the use of political power or legal coercion. The temptation to do so has often been—and in some cases still is—especially acute in Orthodox countries. One of the more morally corrosive aspects of modern democratic politics is the tendency to slander and revile—even, in fact, to demonize—others with whom one does not agree. Indeed, there is no other space than in the political, perhaps, where the modern Christian must strive more assiduously against the prevailing tendencies of the age, and seek instead to obey the commandment of love. Orthodox Christians should support the language of human rights, not because it is a language fully adequate to all that God intends for his creatures, but because it preserves a sense of the inviolable uniqueness of every person, and of the priority of human goods over national interests, while providing a legal and ethical grammar upon which all parties can, as a rule, arrive at certain basic agreements. It is a language intended to heal divisions in those political communities in which persons of widely differing beliefs must coexist. It allows for a general practice and ethos of honoring each person's infinite and inherent dignity (a dignity, of course, that the Church sees as the effect of God's image in all human beings). Orthodox Christians must recognize that a language of common social accord, one that insists upon the inviolability of human dignity and freedom, is needed for the preservation and promotion of a just society; and the language of human rights has the power to accomplish this with admirable clarity. Neither, certainly, should Orthodox Christians fear the reality of cultural and social pluralism. Indeed, they should rejoice in the dynamic confluence of human cultures in the modern world, which is one of the special glories of our age, and take it as a blessing that all human cultures, in all their variety and beauty, are coming more and more to occupy the same civic and political spaces. The Church must in fact support those government policies and laws that best promote such pluralism. More than that, it must thank God for the riches of all the world's many cultures, and for the gracious gift of their peaceful coexistence in modern societies.

§13   Ours is, it is often said, a secular age. This is not to say, of course, that religion has faded from all societies. In some of them, in fact, it remains as potent a cultural force as it ever was. And, even in the most thoroughly laicized and secularized nations of the West, religious belief and practice remain far livelier than one would expect if the religious impulse were merely an accidental aspect of human culture. But the constitutions of most modern states, even those that formally recognize an established church, assume the civic priority of a public space devoid of religious associations, and of a political order free from ecclesiastical authority. Many today, in fact, believe that democratic society is possible only to the degree that religion has been relegated to the private sphere entirely, and allowed no role in the articulation of policy. This is, of course, an unreasonable demand, and one that becomes despotic if enforced by coercive legal means. Human ethical convictions do not evolve in conceptual vacuums, and religious adherence is an inseparable part of how a great many communities and individuals come to have any notions at all of the common good, moral community, and social responsibility. To silence the voice of faith in the public sphere is also to silence the voice of conscience for a great many citizens, and to exclude them from civic life altogether. At the same time, however, the dissolution of the ancient compact between state and church—or throne and altar—has also been a great blessing for Christian culture. It has freed the Church from what was all too frequently a slavish and unholy submission to earthly power and a complicity in its evils. It is, in fact, very much in the interest of the Church that the institutional association of Christianity with the interests of the state be as tenuous as possible, not because the Church seeks to withdraw from society at large, but because it is called to proclaim the Gospel to the world and to serve God in all things, uncompromised by alliance with worldly ambitions. The Orthodox Church, then, should be thankful that God has providentially allowed for the reduction of the Church's political enfranchisement in most of the lands of ancient Christendom, so that it may more faithfully conduct and promote its mission to all nations and persons. Certainly, the Church can be at peace quite happily with a political order that does not impose theological conformity upon its people by coercive means, as such an order allows the Church to make a far purer and more immediate appeal to the reason and conscience of everyone.

§14   In no sense does this preclude the Church from direct and robust cooperation with political and civil authorities and organs of state in advancing the common good and pursuing works of charity. Christianity began as a minority religious movement within an imperial culture either indifferent or hostile to its presence. Even then, in times of distress, such as periods of plague or famine, Christians often distinguished themselves by the selflessness of their service to their neighbors. And, throughout the early centuries of the faith, the Church's provisions for the desperate—widows and orphans especially, who were often the most indigent and imperiled persons of the ancient world—made it the first organized institution of social welfare in Western society. After the conversion of the empire to Christianity, moreover, there was no more significant change to the legal and social constitution of imperial society than the immense expansion of the Church's philanthropic resources and social responsibility. No general characterization of the relation of Church and state in the period of the Christian empire is possible; the alliance bore fruit both good and bad; but no one should doubt the immense improvement in the Western conception of the common good that was inaugurated in—and that slowly, fitfully unfolded from—the introduction of Christian conscience into the social grammar of the late antique world. In time, this cooperation for the sake of the common good was enshrined within Orthodox tradition under the term *"symphonia"* in the Emperor Justinian's Novellas.[12] This same principle was operative in the constitution of many Orthodox nation states in the post-Ottoman period. And today, as well, the principle of *symphonia* can continue to guide the Church in her attempts to work with governments toward the common good and to struggle against injustice. It cannot, however, be invoked as a justification for the imposition of religious orthodoxy on society at large, or for promotion of the Church as a political power. Rather, it should serve to remind Christians that this commitment to the common good—as opposed

---

12   See Justinian, *Novella* 6, 35.27-21. See *The Novels of Justinian: A Complete Annotated English Translation*, vol. 1, Cambridge: Cambridge University Press, 2018.

to the mere formal protection of individual liberties, partisan interests, and the power of corporations—is the true essence of a democratic political order. Without the language of the common good at the center of social life, democratic pluralism all too easily degenerates into pure individualism, free market absolutism, and a spiritually corrosive consumerism.

III. THE COURSE OF HUMAN LIFE

Sanctify our souls and bodies,
and grant that we may worship you in holiness
all the days of our lives

§15 The course of a human life on earth—if it reaches its natural conclusion—begins in the moment of conception in the womb, extends from childhood to adulthood, and culminates at last in the sleep of bodily death. But the stages of human life differ for each soul, and every path that any given person might take, whether chosen or unchosen, leads to possibilities either of sanctity or of spiritual slavery. And in each life the opportunities for ascetic self-denial in service of God's love, and for the work of transfiguring creation, are unique. The proper end of every life well-lived is that of *seeing God face to face*, of *theosis: Beloved,* *1 Corinthians 13:12* *we are God's children now; it does not yet appear what we shall be, but we know that when he appears we shall be like him, for we shall see him as he is.* Yet the journey each person takes *1 John 3:2* through life is also beset by temptations, most especially the temptation to follow those paths that lead only to one's own advantages or aggrandizements rather than to expressions of love for God and solidarity with neighbor.

The Church seeks to accompany the Christian soul all along its way in this world, providing not only counsel but also the means of achieving holiness. And, at every stage, the Church proposes diverse models of life in Christ, diverse vocations for Christian living embraced within the one supreme vocation to seek the Kingdom of God and its justice.

§16   The Orthodox Church's reverence for God's image, even in the smallest among us, is expressed not only in the baptism of infants, but also in their immediate admission to the Eucharist. There could be no greater sacramental affirmation of Christ's instruction to his disciples to find the truest model of life in God's Kingdom in the innocence of children. Christ himself entered the world by way of his mother's womb, and passed through both infancy and childhood, growing in wisdom and stature. Every aspect of human life has been sanctified and glorified in having been assumed by the eternal Son of God; but, in becoming subject to the fragility and dependency of infancy and childhood, the Son revealed with a very special emphasis the astonishing magnitude of God's self-outpouring love in the work of salvation. The innocence of children is, therefore, a thing of extraordinary holiness, a sign of the life of the Kingdom graciously present in our very midst, and must be the object of the Church's ceaseless concern and diligence. The protection and care of children is the most basic and most essential index of any society's dedication to the good. As Christ warned us, *whoever causes one of these little ones who believe in me to sin, it would be better for him to have a great millstone fastened round his neck and to be drowned in the depth of the sea.* Sins against the innocence of

Matthew 19:14, Mark 10:14–16, Luke 18:16–17

Luke 2:52

Matthew 18:6; cf. Mark 9:42, Luke 17:2

children are sins of an especially loathsome kind. No offense against God is worse than is the sexual abuse of children, and none more intolerable to the conscience of the Church. All members of Christ's body are charged with the protection of the young against such violation, and there is no situation in which a member of the Church, on learning of any case of the sexual abuse of a child, may fail immediately to report it to the civil authorities and to the local bishop. Moreover, every faithful Christian is no less bound to expose those who would conceal such crimes from public knowledge or shield them from legal punishment. Neither should any priest ever grant absolution to the perpetrator of such a crime until the latter has surrendered himself or herself to criminal prosecution. The Church is called also to strive for the protection of children around the globe who are—even in an era in which childhood mortality and disease are in decline globally—still subject in many places to war, enslavement, destitution, child labor, and (in the special case of young girls) arranged marriages, often as child brides. So long as these conditions persist in any part of the world, the Church cannot rest in its efforts to end them, by appeal to government authorities, by charitable aid, by assistance in systems of adoption, and by advocacy on behalf of these little ones. It is also the Church's responsibility to work everywhere for the general improvement of childhood conditions in places where there is insufficient access to clean water, good medical care, vaccinations, and other basic necessities. At no time can the Church cease to make clear to all children that they are known and loved by God, or fail to celebrate the exceptional charisms of childhood: spontaneous joy, curiosity, imagination, and trust. Indeed, as Christ taught us, adults should learn to emulate children in these natural gifts: *Whoever humbles*

Matthew 18:4 *himself like this child, he is the greatest in the Kingdom of heaven.*

§17   In our time, as has never before been the case, children are exposed throughout their waking hours to a host of electronic devices and mass media, dedicated in large part to the promotion of unremitting material acquisition. As His-All Holiness Ecumenical Patriarch Bartholomew stated in his 2016 Proclamation of Christmas:

> A child's soul is altered by the influential consump-
> tion of electronic media, especially television and the
> internet, and by the radical transformation of com-
> munication. Unbridled economics transforms them,
> from a young age, into consumers, while the pursuit
> of pleasure rapidly causes their innocence to vanish.

The Church and parents must remember always that de-sires are shaped in childhood, and with them character. It is a gross dereliction to allow children to become so absorbed in a world of fleeting materialist fascinations and trivial material appetites as to leave their deeper ca-pacities for love, selflessness, reverence, generosity, joy in simple things, and indifference to personal possessions undeveloped. Christ called his followers to imitate the guilelessness of children, but much of late modern capi-talist culture seeks to rob children of precisely this pre-cious virtue, and to convert them instead into engines of sheer covetous longing. To protect children against this profound perversion of their created natures is one of the most urgent responsibilities incumbent upon adult Chris-tians in the age of mass communication. St. John Chrysos-tom advises parents that they serve as "gatekeepers of the senses" for their children.[13] A gatekeeper is not a tyrant, as Chrysostom makes clear; but, in controlling a child's access to the world, the gatekeeper endows him or her with the ability to govern his or her own appetites in later life. And this role of gatekeeping may be more important today than ever before, given how completely our senses can be overwhelmed by the incessant din and spectacle of modern mass media.

§18   In most pre-modern societies, the period of childhood was succeeded directly by adulthood, and with it in most cases a life of labor. In our time, increasingly, we have come to think of the transition between childhood and adulthood as an intermediate period, and not necessarily a brief one. Many young adults, for instance, wait some time before detaching themselves from their childhood households and setting out upon independent paths to discern their vocation, and in many cases wait even longer before marrying, having children, and establishing households of their own. As with all large social changes, this reality comes with both privileges and perils. The principal benefit of allowing the young a longer interval in which to discern what their own peculiar gifts and vocations might be is that it liberates them from too great a sense of fated careers. The principal danger is that, in some, this period of decision will become a habit of indecision, even procrastination, and therefore an unnaturally prolonged condition of dependency, immaturity, and uncertainty. Here the Church must be ready to offer counsel and encouragement to young adults: to urge

---

13   John Chrysostom, *On Vainglory and the Right Way for Parents to Bring Up Their Children* 27. See Sources Chrétiennes 188, Paris: Cerf, 1972, 114.

them to advance into life with faith, but also to do so pru-
dently and prayerfully, seriously seeking to discover the
particular gifts God has given them for the work of transfiguring a fallen world and serving God's justice and mercy among others. The Church must be acutely conscious
that it is at this stage of human life that sexuality and the
shape of sexual longing become special concerns, and in
many cases a cause of consternation and even confusion.
In itself, this is nothing new in the human condition, but
ours is an age in which sexuality has become yet another
area of life colonized by the logic of consumerism and
the dynamics of the market. Sexuality has today, in fact,
become as much a consumer strategy or consumer prod-
uct—tantalizing in its fluidity and pervasiveness—as an
innate dimension of human personality. The Church and
the community of the faithful must offer young adults a
vision of sexual relations as life-giving and transfiguring:
an intimate union of body, mind, and spirit, sanctified by
holy matrimony. The body is *a temple of the Holy Spirit with-*
1 Corinthians 6:19   *in you,* and even in its sexual nature is called to exhibit the
sanctity of God's dwelling place.

§19   We live in an age in which sexuality has come more and
more to be understood as a personal fate, and even a private matter. A great many political and social debates in
the modern world turn upon the distinct demands and
needs of heterosexual, homosexual, bisexual, and other
sexual "identities." It is true, as a simple physiological and
psychological fact, that the nature of individual sexual
longing is not simply a consequence of private choice regarding such matters; many of the inclinations and long-
ings of the flesh and the heart to a great extent come into

the world with us, and are nourished or thwarted—accepted or obstructed—in us at an early age. It must be accounted, moreover, a basic right of any person—which no state or civil authority may presume to violate—to remain free from persecution or legal disadvantage as a result of his or her sexual orientation. But the Church understands human identity as residing primarily not in one's sexuality or in any other private quality, but rather in the image and likeness of God present in all of us.[14] All Christians are called always to seek the image and likeness of God in each other, and to resist all forms of discrimination against their neighbors, regardless of sexual orientation. Christians are called to lives of sexual continence, both inside and outside of marriage, precisely on account of the sanctity of sexual life in the created order. But Christians are never called to hatred or disdain for anyone.

§20   As an Orthodox Christian enters adulthood, he or she will begin to follow one of three possible paths: married life, monastic life, or single life. While the three paths may differ in expression, they share the Christian calling in essence as the radical acceptance of love and sharing. Traditionally, Orthodoxy has tended to recognize only two states—the monastic and the married—but it would be a profound dereliction of pastoral responsibility for the Church to fail to acknowledge that, while the single life was very much a rarity in earlier generations, cultural and social changes in the modern age have now made it considerably more common. Some persons may tread more than one of these paths in the course of his or her life; for

---

14   See Assembly of Orthodox Bishops in Germany, *A Letter from the Bishops of the Orthodox Church in Germany to Young People concerning Love, Sexuality, and Marriage,* 2017.

instance, a widowed man or woman might elect to take monastic vows. For most, however, there is only one path to follow, and it is upon that path that he or she is called to serve God's Kingdom and to seek union with God. In the early Church, it was the path of consecrated virginity (which, in time, became the practice of monasticism) that enjoyed the highest esteem. But the Church also in time came to understand marriage as a sacrament, and even condemned hostility to it.[15] There has been at many times in the history of the Church something of a tension between the married life and monasticism, at least as regards their relative spiritual merits. In large part, this was the result of an earlier, pre-Christian understanding of marriage; it was also the result, however, of the unfortunate reality that, until fairly recently in Eastern Christian tradition, spiritual teachings on these matters have been advanced principally by celibate men with no experience of the married life. It is time to put these pernicious prejudices aside and to recognize that marriage is much more than a cultural institution or merely a means for propagating and preserving the human race. If that were all that it is, scripture would not use nuptial imagery as the principal means of describing the sacramental and eschatological union of Christ and his Church. According to scripture, Christ vouchsafed his followers the first of his ministry's signs of divinity at the Wedding Feast in Cana. By contrast, the celibate life appears in the New Testament as having at most a practical value. Marriage is the sacrament of love, or human love raised into the world of the sacramental. It is the only sacrament that involves

---

15   Notably at the Council of Gangra in 340 AD. PL 67.55D.

two persons freely and equally bound one to the other by God. Mystically, man and woman, husband and wife, become one, as the rite of matrimony says: "Yoke them in oneness of mind; crown them into one flesh." The Church took the institution of marriage—which had previously been a relationship understood largely in proprietary and legal terms, concerned principally with domestic and familial economy—and transfigured it into an indissoluble bond between persons that mystically signifies the love of Christ for his Church. It is a bond that, among other things, makes the fullness of human nature, in all its fruitfulness, present in a single shared life. For, while the full image of God dwells in each of us severally, the "image of humanity" is divided in us between man and woman. It is a bond also that intertwines formerly separate individual spiritual efforts into a shared vocation to transfigure the fallen world, and to tread the path toward *theosis* in Christ. None of our works of love in this life is ever undertaken in isolation, of course; each of them necessarily involves an orientation away from ourselves and toward our neighbor. But, in the context of marriage, the very idea of the "neighbor" takes on new meaning, as the married life involves two persons entering together upon a single ascetical course, one in which they must sacrifice each for the other as a matter of mere daily existence, and must subject themselves to one another. In a sense, husband and *Ephesians 5:21* wife become one conjugal being, as is stated in Genesis 2:24 and as is affirmed by Christ: *'For this reason a man shall leave his father and mother and be joined to his wife, and the two shall become one flesh.' So they are no longer two but one flesh.* *Matthew 19:5–6; Mark 10:7–8*

§21   An increasing number of Orthodox marriages today include a spouse who is not an Orthodox Christian. These unions may involve very different challenges than those encountered by two Orthodox spouses, but they too should be understood as constituting a shared effort toward the transfiguration of the world and union with God. As the Orthodox Church finds itself in lands of increasingly diverse populations, marriages between Orthodox and non-Orthodox will certainly require the Church's most careful pastoral attention, as is stated in the document entitled "The Sacrament of Marriage and its Impediments" of the Holy and Great Council:

> With the salvation of man as the goal, the possibility of the exercise of ecclesiastical *oikonomia* in relation to impediments to marriage must be considered by the Holy Synod of each autocephalous Orthodox Church according to the principles of the holy canons and in a spirit of pastoral discernment.[16]

Although twenty centuries separate us from the time of the Apostle Paul, our situation may be not all that different from that of the Corinthian Christian community to whom he sent instructions on this very issue: *For the unbelieving husband is consecrated through his wife, and the unbelieving wife is consecrated through her husband.*

1 Corinthians 7:14

§22   All marriages—whether the spouses be Orthodox, non-Orthodox, or both—are marred by the effects of sin. Precisely because it is a place of such immense responsibility, emotional commitment, and intimate relations, the family is also a place where the most shattering kinds of mental, physical, sexual, and emotional abuse can occur.

---

16   Section II.5.ii.

The Orthodox Church recognizes that the principal moral responsibility of the adults in a dysfunctional household is the protection of the family's most vulnerable members, and acknowledges that in many cases only the end of a marriage can assure the physical safety and spiritual health of everyone involved. One of the lamentable realities of life in our broken world is that marital life is sometimes ruptured beyond repair. In a very real way, divorce is more than a consequence of our brokenness as fallen creatures; it is a markedly vivid expression of it. But divorce does not preclude the possibility of healing for the parties involved, or shut off their path of deification. Thus, the Church also allows for remarriage, albeit acknowledging in its rite for second marriage that this is an accommodation, not an ideal. The Sixth Ecumenical Council advised a period of penance for the divorced and remarried of as many as seven years before readmission to the Eucharist (Canon 37), though the Council in Trullo added to this prescription the qualification that, in cases of abandonment of one spouse by the other, the abandoned party could forgo penance altogether (Canon 87). On these grounds, in its pastoral and paternal concern for clergy who care for the community, the Ecumenical Patriarchate has recently further considered exceptions to the canons regarding the remarriage of divorced clergy. In general, though, no single rule for penitential reconciliation with the Church has ever been imposed universally. Given the uniqueness of each person and distinctiveness of every marriage, the Church must offer compassionate counsel to the divorced, appropriate to the special circumstances of each.

§23   The marriage rite includes many petitions for the eventual bearing of children, including the Psalmist's prayer that the newly married couple will live to see their "children's children." Some of the children who enrich the new household created by a marriage may be the fruit of the couple's sexual union, while others may be adopted, and still others may be fostered; but all are equally welcome within the sanctuary of the family and the body of the Church. Parenthood is a distinctively privileged symbol of love's transfiguring power, as well as of God's love for his creatures. Moreover, the blessing of children brings with it the vocation of the family as a whole to create a kind of polity, a microcosm emblematic of a redeemed creation, and therefore also a place of hospitality for those outside its immediate circle. Moreover, while true love is always fruitful, this fruitfulness is not only expressed through children; it can also be manifested through the diverse gifts of the Spirit: through hospitality, through service, and through common creative efforts of countless kinds. Yet none of this is easily achieved. Children are a glorious blessing, but in the fallen world every blessing is haunted by the curse of Adam and Eve. Parenthood too is a field of ascetic labor, not only because parents must sacrifice their own interests for those of their children (which can be a great joy in itself), but because parents must also endure the sufferings and fears and sadnesses of their children, or recognize at times their own failures in raising their children; and sometimes, like the Mother of God herself, parents must endure the loss of a son or daughter, which is a pain greater than any other that life can bring, and *Luke 2:32* which pierces the soul like a sword. Ideally, of course, both parents will be present all through the rearing of their children; but sometimes, as a result of death, divorce, or other misfortunes, the task falls to one parent alone. In these circumstances, the Church has a special responsibility, as the family of Christ's body, to lend its solace and support—material, emotional, and spiritual. Moreover, the Church should extend the sacramental gift of baptism to all children, irrespective of the manner in which they were conceived or adopted.

§24   It is not the case that a man and a woman united in sacramental marriage become "one flesh" only in the bearing of children, even if (historically speaking) that may have been the chief connotation of the term as it was employed in the book of Genesis. From a very early period, Orthodox tradition has affirmed the sacramental completeness of every marriage that the Church blesses, even those that do not produce offspring. As St. John Chrysostom observed, "But suppose there is no child; do they remain two and not one? No; their intercourse effects the joining of their bodies, and they are made one, just as when perfume is mixed with ointment."[17] The Church anticipates, of course, that most marriages will be open to conception; but it also understands that there are situations in which spiritual, physical, psychological, or financial impediments arise that make it wise—at least, for a time—to delay or forego the bearing of children. The Orthodox Church has no dogmatic objection to the use of safe and non-abortifacient contraceptives within the context of married life, not as an ideal or as a permanent arrangement, but as a

17   John Chrysostom, *On Colossians* 12.5. PG 62.388C. See *On Marriage and Family Life*, Crestwood, NY: St. Vladimir's Seminary Press, 2003, 76.

provisional concession to necessity. The sexual union of a couple is an intrinsic good that serves to deepen the love of each for the other and their devotion to a shared life. By the same token, the Church has no objection to the use of certain modern and still-evolving reproductive technologies for couples who earnestly desire children, but who are unable to conceive without aid. But the Church cannot approve of methods that result in the destruction of "supernumerary" fertilized ova. The necessary touchstone for assessing whether any given reproductive technology is licit must be the inalienable dignity and incomparable value of every human life. As medical science in this area continues to advance, Orthodox Christians—lay believers and clergy alike—must consult this touchstone in every instance in which a new method appears for helping couples to conceive and bear children, and must also consider whether that method honors the sacred relationship between the two spouses.

§25   Orthodox tradition, on the Feast of the Annunciation, celebrates the conception of Christ in his mother's womb, and on the Feast of the Visitation recalls John the Baptist leaping with joy in his mother's womb at the sound of the voice of the pregnant Mother of God. Already in the womb each of us is a spiritual creature, a person formed in God's image and created to rejoice in God's presence. From the first generations of Christians, therefore, the Church has abhorred the practice of elective abortion as infanticide. As early as the *Didache*, the first-century record of Church practices and ordinances, rejection of abortion was an express principle of the new faith,[18] one that—alongside the

---

18   *Didache* 2. See *Early Christian Writings: The Apostolic Fathers*, London: Penguin Classics, 1987 [revised].

rejection of infant-exposure and capital punishment—
demonstrated that Christian confession was opposed to
the taking of human life, even in those cases in which pagan culture had regarded it as licit or even necessary. A
human being is more than the gradually emergent result
of a physical process; life begins at the moment of conception. A child's claim upon our moral regard then is
absolute from that first moment, and Christians are forbidden from shedding innocent blood at every stage of
human development. The Church recognizes, of course,
that pregnancies are often terminated as a result of poverty, despair, coercion, or abuse, and it seeks to provide
a way of reconciliation for those who have succumbed to
these terrible pressures. Inasmuch, however, as the act of
abortion is always objectively a tragedy, one that takes an
innocent human life, reconciliation must involve the acknowledgment of this truth before complete repentance,
reconciliation, and healing are possible. Moreover, the
Church must be ready at all times—inasmuch as it truly
wishes to affirm the goodness of every life—to come to
the aid of women in situations of unintended pregnancy, whether as the result of rape or of consensual sexual
union, and to come also to the aid of expectant mothers
suffering from penury, abuse, or other adverse conditions, by providing them material and emotional support,
spiritual succor, and every assurance of God's love, both
during and after pregnancy.

§26   In the Orthodox marriage rite, the Church prays that the
newly married couple might "be made glad with the sight
of sons and daughters." The joy thus anticipated is unqualified; it is elicited not only by infants or children who

meet a specific standard of fitness or health. All children are known and loved by God, all are bearers of his image and likeness, and all are due the same respect, reverence, and care. In the eyes of the Church, each of us is born as *John 9:3* we are, *so that the works of God might be made manifest in [us].* Therefore, the Orthodox Church recognizes no legitimate resort to the eugenic termination of new human life; and it welcomes every new medical advance that can preserve and improve the lives of children afflicted by disease and disability. The Church does recognize, however, that in the course of some pregnancies there arise tragic and insoluble medical situations in which the life of the unborn child cannot be preserved or prolonged without grave danger to the life of the mother, and that the only medical remedy may result in or hasten the death of the unborn child, contrary to all that the parents had desired. In such situations, the Church cannot pretend to be competent to know the best way of proceeding in every instance, and must commend the matter to the prayerful deliberations of parents and their physicians. It can, however, offer counsel, as well as prayers for the healing and salvation of all the lives involved. Furthermore, the Church laments the ubiquity of the loss of life *in utero* through miscarriage and stillbirth, understanding these experiences as particularly powerful forms of bereavement for the family, and it must revise those of its prayers that suggest otherwise, and rise to the sensitive and loving pastoral care that loss of pregnancy requires.

§27   Another path of the Christian through this world is that of the monastic life. Since the Church's earliest years, men and women have assembled together in order to pursue a life of prayer, and have done so in varying degrees of community or seclusion. By removing themselves from society, partly or wholly, they remind themselves and others that the Kingdom of God is not of this world. As every Christian is meant to do, they prophetically recall and persistently remind us that *we look to the city which is to come* and "look [forward] to . . . the life of the age to come" *Hebrews 13:14* (Nicene-Constantinopolitan Creed); but they do so with a special charism and with a very particular intensity. Their withdrawal from ordinary social commerce may seem at times to contradict the commandment of love for one's neighbor; but every change wrought by the grace of God, even in the secret place of the heart, benefits the whole universe. St. Silouan the Athonite said that, "to pray for others is to shed blood."[19] And monasteries often also serve the larger world by preparing a place apart from earthly cares, into which the enclosed can then often welcome the laity, so as to offer them spiritual guidance and periods of refuge from the troubles and temptations of ordinary life. This is much more than mere physical hospitality; in the words of St. Maria Skobtsova:

> If someone turns with his spiritual world toward the spiritual world of another person, he encounters an awesome and inspiring mystery . . . He comes into contact with the true image of God in man, with the very icon of God incarnate in the world, with a reflection of the mystery of God's incarnation and divine manhood.[20]

---

19 Archimandrite Sophrony (Sakharov), *St. Silouan the Athonite*, Stavropegic Monastery of St. John the Baptist: Essex, 1991, 240.

20 Maria Skobtsova, "The Second Gospel Commandment," *Mother Maria Skobtsova: Essential Writings*, Maryknoll, NY: Orbis Books, 2002, 57.

Monastic celibacy, moreover, implies no denigration of the sexual union proper to married life. Rather, it constitutes a special exercise of charity and forgiveness. The monastic life is always an act of thanksgiving, and so has the regular celebration of the Eucharist at its center. It is also a corporate discipline of communal generosity, shared prayer, and mutual forgiveness. In this way, the monastic life foreshadows God's Kingdom, perhaps no more truly than the life of the Christian family, but in a distinctive mode and according to a very particular and holy form of communal self-renunciation. It is never reducible to mere self-serving introversion or self-centered isolation. Though the monastic is not sacramentally and spiritually bound to a single person in the way that a married person is, the monastic does experience and express a profound degree of personal love, directed toward others and toward God. "A true monk weeps for the sins of each of his brothers [and sisters] and rejoices over the progress of each," says St. John Climacus.[21]

§28   A third path of life, that of the adult who neither marries nor becomes a monastic, is sometimes a consciously chosen path, taken for any number of reasons particular to the individual, but at other times is a matter of mere circumstance. Certain persons are neither called to the monastic life, nor able or inclined to find a spouse. Such persons, however, are no less a part of the whole family of Christ's body, and no less able to contribute to the world's sanctification. Indeed, they often possess special gifts of discernment, personal discipline, and spiritual insight that persons absorbed in the daily business of familial life

---

21   John Climacus, *Ladder of Divine Ascent*, Step 4.47. PG 88.705A.

cannot readily cultivate. In every case all single laypersons are called to the same life of charity, and enjoy the same dignity as God's beloved children. The Church must recognize, however, how difficult a vocation this will often prove. The married person may rely for support upon his or her spouse, the monastic upon his or her fellow renunciants. The single lay person often has no one as such on whom to rely in anything like a comparable measure. Holy friendship is a source of spiritual comfort and strength in many single lives; but it does not necessarily suffice to alleviate the loneliness of those who tread this particular path. Here Orthodox tradition provides somewhat scant traditional and pastoral resources; but, as the numbers of single laypersons continue to grow, the Church must seek to evolve pastoral practices adequate to their needs.

§29   All the paths of adulthood are open equally to every individual, and in each the Orthodox Church affirms the full equality and dignity of each human person created in the image and likeness of God. While the Church acknowledges that men and women have different life experiences, and incarnate human nature in distinct fashions, it must reject any suggestion that one surpasses the other in spiritual dignity. As St. Basil noted of men and women: "The natures are alike of equal honor, the virtues are equal, the struggle equal, the judgment alike."[22] And as St. Gregory the Theologian affirmed: "The same Creator for man and woman, for both of them the same clay, the same image, the same law, the same death, and the

---

22   Basil of Caesarea, Discourse 1, 18: On the Origin of Humanity, in *On the Human Condition*, Crestwood, NY: St Vladimir's Seminary Press, 45.

same resurrection."[23] That said, the inequality of men and women in almost every sphere of life is one of the tragic realities of our fallen world. In fact, while the Orthodox Church has always held as a matter of doctrine and theology that men and women are equals in personhood, it has not always proved scrupulously faithful to this ideal. The Church has, for instance, for far too long retained in her prayers and Eucharistic practices ancient and essentially superstitious prejudices about purity and impurity in regard to women's bodies, and has even allowed the idea of ritual impurity to attach itself to childbirth. Yet no Christian woman who has prepared herself for communion through prayer and fasting should be discouraged from approaching the chalice. The Church must also remain attentive to the promptings of the Spirit in regard to the ministry of women, especially in our time, when many of the most crucial offices of ecclesial life—theologians, seminary professors, canonists, readers, choir directors, and experts in any number of professions that benefit the community of faith—are occupied by women in increasingly great numbers; and the Church must continue to consider how women can best participate in building up the body of Christ, including a renewal of the order of the female diaconate for today.

§30   Each of these paths of life has its own distinctive stages; but all paths end—unless they are prematurely obviated—in the same final stages of old age and death. The aged in the community of the faith merit a special reverence from the faithful, for the wisdom they have acquired and for the perseverance in faith that they have demonstrated. As

---

23   Gregory the Theologian, *Discourse* 37.6. PG 36.289C.

they age, however, they become increasingly vulnerable to illness and disability. Even this challenge can provide an opportunity for deepened humility and growth in faith, both for those who are aging and for their caregivers; but it is also a responsibility that the rest of the body of Christ must never shirk. And, in the modern world, this poses special difficulties and demands for many communities. Modern society seems to have less and less time for the elderly, and seems ever more disposed to consign them to care facilities out of sight and out of mind. In the late capitalist world, old age—once recognized as something venerable—is often treated as something of an embarrassment, and the elderly as something of a burden and a nuisance. The Orthodox Church teaches that there are no limits to the innate spiritual dignity of the person, no matter how the body or the mind may be afflicted by the passage of the years. The Church must require of any just society that it provide adequately for the elderly, and make sure that they are not subjected to neglect, mistreatment, or destitution. And it charges the community of the faithful to make every effort to care for and learn from its oldest members.

§31   Each of these paths of human life reaches its end on earth sooner or later. In the Divine Liturgy of St. John Chrysostom, the Church defines a "good, Christian ending to our lives" as "peaceful, without shame or pain," and prays that all Christians might know it as such. In other prayers, it expresses the hope that the dying might leave this life secure in the knowledge that they are treasured, for even the sparrows cannot fall without God seeing them. Death *Matthew 10:29* is a terrible prospect in itself, the enemy whom God has conquered in Christ but who nonetheless, this side of the Kingdom, still comes to seize us all. At times, its approach evokes despair. At other times, some of us flee to its embrace out of a still deeper despair. Suicide has always been understood in the Orthodox Church as a tragedy and as a profound assault upon the dignity of the human person. But, over time, as mental illness and emotional fragility have come to be better understood, the Church has increasingly acknowledged that suicide typically involves "spiritual and/or physiological factors that significantly compromise a person's rationality and freedom."[24] This being so, Christian love dictates that Church burial and full services for a person who has taken his or her own life should not be presumptively refused, nor should the faithful regard the person who dies by suicide as someone who has willingly and consciously rejected God. This is a case of divine economy and compassion informing sacramental and pastoral economy. Here the antique prejudices of the tradition should be corrected by the superior diagnostic and therapeutic discoveries of the modern age. Still, suicide can never become the permissible solution to worldly suffering. Even for those enduring terrible illnesses, one must not hasten death, however merciful it might seem to do so; the image of God remains inviolable even in its last days in this world. Euthanasia is alien to the Christian vision of life. That said, it is perfectly permissible for those who are dying to refuse extraordinary medical treatments and technologies that artificially prolong bodily life long past the

---

24 Standing Conference of the Canonical Orthodox Bishops in the Americas, *Pastoral Letter on Suicide*, 2007.

point when the body would have naturally yielded up the spirit. It is not incumbent on a Christian to protract the sufferings of the flesh out of terror of the inevitable, or to cling to this world beyond reason. Death in the grace of God need not be feared. The Orthodox Church comforts those who mourn, grieves with those whose loved ones have departed from this life, and prays for the dead; but, more importantly, Orthodox Christians "look forward to the resurrection of the dead and the life of the age to come" (Nicene-Constantinopolitan Creed). We look to the time when our ascetical struggles in this life will bear their final, true fruit in the next, when all our efforts to transfigure the world are fulfilled in a renewed creation, and when our journey of *theosis* will be carried up into eternity as we are *transformed from glory to glory.*[25]   *2 Corinthians 3:18*

IV. POVERTY, WEALTH, AND CIVIL JUSTICE

Remember, Lord, those who are mindful of the poor

§32   When the eternal Son became human, divesting himself of his divine glory and exchanging the "form of God" for the *form of a servant,* he elected thereby to identify himself   *Philippians 2:6–7* with the most marginal, politically powerless, and socially disadvantaged persons of his age. Born among a subject people without any legal rights before their imperial colonizers, raised in a household belonging to the lowly artisanal class, Christ began his mission in the hinterlands of the Galilee and devoted his ministry chiefly to the most abjectly destitute and hopeless of his people. In this, he took up the mission of the prophets of Israel, and indeed

---

25   See Gregory of Nyssa, *On Perfection*. PG 46.285C.

the deepest moral cause of the whole of the Law and the Prophets. In inaugurating his public ministry, he took the proclamation of the prophet Isaiah as his own: *The Spirit of the Lord is upon me, because he has anointed me to preach good news to the poor. He has sent me to proclaim release to the captives and recovering of sight to the blind, to set at liberty those who the* Luke 4:18–19 *oppressed, to proclaim the acceptable year of the Lord.* And this special commitment to the dispossessed and desperate, far from being merely an incidental element of his mission to the children of Israel, defined its very essence. To Luke 20:46–47 those who profited from the exploitation of the weak, or Luke 6:24–25; 16:25 who ignored the plight of the poor, his warnings could not have been more dire or his condemnations more uncompromising. His demands upon the good will and private substance of his followers, moreover, were unremitting where the needs of the destitute were concerned. He commanded them to give without reserve to *all* who might Matthew 5:42 beg from them, with so graceful a largesse one hand Matthew 6:3 would be unconscious of the other's generosity, and forbade them to reserve any of their wealth for themselves as Matthew 6:19–20 earthly treasures. Not only did he instruct the rich young ruler to sell all his possessions and give the proceeds to Matthew 19:16–30; Mark 10:17–31; the poor; he demanded the same of all who wished to at-Luke 18:18–30 tach themselves to him and considered no one who failed Luke 12:33 to give all to the needy worthy to be his disciple. Indeed, Luke 14:33 he left no doubt what was required of those who hoped to enter God's Kingdom: *Come, you that are blessed by my Father, inherit the Kingdom prepared for you from the foundation of the world; for I was hungry and you gave me food, I was thirsty and you gave me drink, I was a stranger and you welcomed me, I was naked and you clothed me, I was sick and visited me, I was in prison and you came to me.* In following his Father's call, moreover, he endured all the extremes of homelessness and rejection: *The Son of Man has nowhere to lay his head; They rose up, drove him out of the city, and led him to the brow of the hill on which their city was built, so that they might hurl him off the cliff.* And he ended his earthly ministry condemned by a foreign occupying power, before whose tribunals he possessed no legal rights, and died the death of the lowliest criminal, executed by the most agonizing and humiliating instruments of capital punishment known to his age.

§33   All this being so, it is impossible for the Church truly to follow Christ or to make him present to the world if it fails to place this absolute concern for the poor and disadvantaged at the very center of its moral, religious, and spiritual life. The pursuit of social justice and civil equity—provision for the poor and shelter for the homeless, protection for the weak, welcome for the displaced, and assistance for the disabled—is not merely an ethos the Church recommends for the sake of a comfortable conscience, but is a necessary means of salvation, the indispensable path to union with God in Christ; and to fail in these responsibilities is to invite condemnation before the judgment seat of God. Thus it was that the earliest Christian communities of the apostolic age adopted a manner of life radically unlike that of the greater culture, holding all possessions in common and surrendering all private wealth to the community as a whole, so that the needs of every member of Christ's body might be met. At that time, it did not lie within the power of the Church to fashion civil society anew; nor could the Church—given

Matthew 25: 34–36

Matthew 8:20; Luke 9:58

Luke 4:29

Matthew 25:41–45

Acts 2:44–45; 4:32–37

the absolutely intractable reality of imperial order—produce anything like an abstract political ideology that might correct or ameliorate the injustices of the age. Nevertheless, Christians were able to care for the poor within their reach, and for widows and orphans especially (the most helpless classes of the ancient world), and to create among themselves a polity of love that left no one to his or her fate. What is more, this understanding of the life in Christ as one of radical solidarity was carried over—not perfectly, unfortunately, but to some real effect—into the age of the politically enfranchised Church. After the conversion of the Emperor Constantine, no change in imperial policy was more significant as a concrete expression of the social consequences of the Gospel than the vast expansion of the Church's provision for the poor, with large material support from the state.

§34   All of the greatest of the Church Fathers of the fourth and fifth centuries, moreover, bore eloquent witness to the deep Christian intuition that life in Christ must entail a militant hostility to the conditions that create poverty, as well as a heroic commitment to philanthropy and charity. St. Basil the Great inveighed against the inequalities of wealth in the society of his day, and excoriated the rich who imagined that they had a right to withhold their goods from others on merely legal grounds; all blessings come from God, he insisted, and all the goods of creation are the common property of humankind.[26] Anyone who exploits the poor for his own profit stores up damnation for himself.[27] Anyone who fails to share his money with the

---

26   Basil, *Homily on "I Will Pull Down My Barns."* Begins at PG 31.261A.

27   Basil, *In Hexaemeron* 7.3. PG 29.152C.

hungry is guilty not merely of a dereliction of a general responsibility, but of murder.[28] St. John Chrysostom said the same of all who gain their wealth from unjust practices that subject the poor to greater poverty.[29] According to him, the rich man who will not share out his wealth to those in need is a thief,[30] for all creation's plenty comes from God and is the common birthright of all persons;[31] anything the rich man possesses has been entrusted to him for the common good,[32] and all he has belongs to all others.[33] St. Ambrose of Milan concurred.[34] This was the age when Christian theologians first had the opportunity—and the obligation—to consider how to translate the Apostolic Church's radical social solidarity and corporate charity into the civic practices of a putatively Christian culture. None of them, it seems, imagined that the Christian moral life could be divided into separate spheres of the private and the public, or that the Gospel's requirements of the consciences of the faithful did not extend to the entirety of a Christian society. All were keenly aware that a Christian culture must address the structural evils that condemn so many to penury while granting immense wealth to a very few. As St. Basil affirmed, human beings are social and political creatures by nature, who

---

28   Basil, *Homily in Times of Famine and Drought* 7. PG 31.321CD.

29   John Chrysostom, *Homilies on Matthew* 5.5. PG 57.60–61.

30   John Chrysostom, *On Lazarus and Dives* 2.4. PG 48.987–988.

31   John Chrysostom, *Homily to the People of Antioch* 2.6. PG 49.43.

32   John Chrysostom, *On the Apostle's Words "Having the Same Spirit."* PG 51.299.

33   John Chrysostom, *Homilies on 1 Corinthians* 10.3. PG 61.85A. And *Homilies on 1 Timothy* 11.2. PG 62.555B.

34   Ambrose, *In Hexaemeron* 6. Begins at PL 14.257A. And *Exposition of Luke's Gospel*, Book 7. Begins at PL 15.1699A.

must share their goods with one another in order to end poverty; and so, he insisted, it is a necessary public policy in a Christian society that a treasury be established from which the basic needs of all might be met and the plenty of creation might be justly redistributed.[35] Nor should such measures be regarded as extraordinary or supererogatory for Christians. According to St. Ambrose, from a Christian perspective such redistribution is no more than the just restitution that the rich owe the poor for their disproportionate share of the common property of the whole of humankind.[36] One great challenge that the Orthodox Church in the modern world cannot fail to meet is that of finding ways to obey these scriptural and patristic teachings and traditions regarding the common good in the present, and it is a challenge that requires both discernment and patience. It also demands, however, an uncompromising fidelity to the person of Christ and to the examples of the apostles and saints. This means that the Church is called to condemn current social conditions where condemnation is warranted, to offer praise where those conditions are praiseworthy, and to encourage change for the better wherever encouragement may bear fruit. Above all, the Church can be no less concerned for the plight of the poor and the defenseless than was Christ himself, and no less ready to speak for them when their voices cannot be heard.

$35   Among the most common evils of all human societies— though often brought to an unprecedented level of refinement and precision in modern developed countries—are

---

35   Basil, *Homilies on the Psalms* 14.1.6. PG 29.263B.

36   Ambrose, *On Naboth the Israelite* 3.11–15. PL14.769B.

the gross inequalities of wealth often produced or abetted by regressive policies of taxation and insufficient regulation of fair wages, which favor the interests of those rich enough to influence legislation and secure their wealth against the demands of the general good. While it is true that imprudent taxation of the private institutions that create jobs *can* in some circumstances depress employment and result in greater burdens for the poor, this is a danger rarely if ever realized in industrialized nations. The far more common reality is one in which the wealthiest members of the investment class are protected against bearing a tax burden proportionate to the benefits they enjoy from their place in society, while corporate entities are allowed to indulge in practices that create markets for cheap labor at the expense of the welfare of workers. The results of this are both a greater burden placed upon the earnings of the working middle classes and, often enough, inadequate public provision for the poor. Against all such practices, surely, the Orthodox Church must insist upon equity and compassion as fundamental principles of tax policy and guidelines for fair wages, as well as upon the moral responsibility of the wealthy to contribute as much as they can to the welfare of society as a whole, and the concomitant responsibility of governments to require that the wealthy do this without unfair legal protections or avenues of evasion. The claims of the Church Fathers that the plenty of creation is the equal birthright to all those created in God's image, and that therefore the wealthiest among us are entrusted and obligated to share their substance with the poor, may run contrary to some of the modern world's most cherished understandings of private property; but they are absolutely essential to a Christian vision of this world as a gracious gift from God, and express a responsibility that in the eyes of the Church is incumbent upon any just society.

$36   Another consequence of laws designed principally to secure the wealth of the wealthy is, of course, the frequent reduction of labor to a commodity, and of laborers to a condition that it is not unfair to describe as "wage slavery." This is especially true in industrialized nations whose laws make it excessively easy for large employers to increase their profit margins at the expense of their employees, by withholding benefits, by failing to provide a living wage, by managing workers' hours in ways that deny them the true privileges of full employment, and above all by making cheap labor into a kind of natural resource to be exploited, particularly in labor markets where basic workers' protections do not exist. Often enough, business practices of this sort are permitted under the shelter of free trade accords, even though the connection of such practices to the larger economics of international free trade is tenuous at best. Global corporations are often able to reduce their expenditures and increase their profits by removing their operations to parts of the world where labor is inexpensive precisely because workers are desperate and local governments are more eager to attract foreign investment than to institute humane labor policies, or even to secure the most basic protections for workers. This has the dual effect of lowering wages in the developed world and fortifying poverty in the developing world. Moreover, at the margins of all labor markets there exist classes of persons who are excluded from the protections of the law and therefore subject to exploitation against which they can make no effective legal appeal: undocumented workers, for instance, who must accept wages far below the legal minimum in exchange for work of the most onerous kinds, or displaced and even quite literally enslaved women from the developing world who are forced into sex-trafficking, along with all the abuse, dangers, and degradations that such a life involves. Moreover, despite certain "populist" claims to the contrary, these evils are often only promoted by inflexible immigration laws and impermeable borders. It is very much in the interest of unprincipled employers that different national labor markets be as segregated from one another as possible, as this has the dual effect of creating a "shadow" labor force of undocumented workers to be exploited within national boundaries and of preserving the existence of depressed labor markets to be exploited beyond those boundaries. An international free flow of labor, and with it the capacity of labor to organize on a global scale and thereby demand basic standards of employment in all labor markets, would make such exploitation very nearly impossible. Hence the unholy collusion between many transnational corporate interests and many states to make the free flow of labor across borders impossible, often by the most draconian means.

$37   Against all such practices, the Orthodox Church will insist upon the high dignity of labor and upon the inviolable sanctity of each person, and that *The laborer is worthy of his hire.* Moreover, no one should labor without respite: *1 Timothy 5:18* the Church insists that a just economy or business is one that insures not only the reasonable productivity and respectable pay of workers, but their opportunities for sufficient rest from work, for recreation, and for restoration of body and soul with their families, friends, and communities. It must require of every society with the means to do so that it protect its workers—both documented and undocumented—against abuse, humiliation, neglect, and cynical exploitation. It must ask of governments that they pass laws that make it possible for employers to provide jobs but not to treat labor as a mere commodity or business expense without any special moral status. Every advanced economy must, if it would be just, make it a matter of law and custom that those businesses that enjoy incorporation in nations that provide trustworthy legal systems, functioning financial institutions, and basic civil freedoms must be willing, as part of their social compact with those nations, to comply with laws and practices that provide workers with humane conditions and living wages, and that forbid complicity in corrupt systems of structural poverty in other nations. This entails laws that ensure that, even in establishing facilities in the developing world, such businesses must be held to the same standards of conduct toward labor that obtain in the developed world; and the ability of businesses to manufacture, market, and trade goods, or otherwise to participate in the global market, must be made contingent upon just labor practices. The Church must also call for laws that do not subject undocumented workers to the terror of legal penalty when seeking redress for abuses on the part of their employers. At the same time, the Church should encourage corporations to invest humanely in depressed parts of the world, and to try to provide opportunities where none previously existed; it asks only that such businesses must be held to standards of conduct that respect the inherent dignity of every human person, and that they make their investments in developing economies in order to improve the conditions of the poor rather than to profit from their poverty.

§38   Most of all, along with St. Basil and St. Ambrose and other of the Fathers, the Orthodox Church must insist upon the responsibility of society to provide a social safety net that genuinely protects the poor and disadvantaged from absolute penury, degradation, homelessness, misery, and despair. All are called to the banquet that God prepares, and all who would feast must *invite the poor, the crippled, the lame, and the blind.* And this is a call to be taken up as   *Luke 14:13* a matter not only of private charity, but of public justice as well. This means, too, that the Church cannot remain silent when such provisions as the laws allow are inadequate to the needs they are intended to address, or fail to secure a reasonable semblance of social and civil equality for their beneficiaries. The Church must especially censure nations that squander an inordinate proportion of the public purse on enterprises that do little but profit or flatter the enfranchised. Especially egregious are examples of social neglect in nations that choose to divert public sums from social welfare to large and needless weapons' programs, whose only real purpose is to reinforce the "military-industrial complex" and enrich those whose business is the ceaseless production of ever more sophisticated and devastating means of killing, waging war, and terrorizing civilian populations. A nation that consistently fails to provide even the most rudimentary level of general health care to its citizens living in poverty and that tolerates the homelessness of its most indigent,

but that simultaneously spends a disproportionate por-
tion of its public revenues each year on military expansion, is a society engaged in practices against which a
properly informed Christian conscience must rebel. And,
though it be impolitic to do so, the Church must be willing
to condemn moral derelictions in the allocation of civic
wealth wherever it sees them.

§39   It should be noted, moreover—especially as it is so
prominent and persistent a motif in the teachings of
Christ—that there is no material mechanism more crucial
for determining who will be wealthy and who poor in any
society than that of inordinate debt. Throughout human
history, arguably, the most essential social division has
always been that between debtors and creditors. A recognition of the fundamental indecency of using interest to
enslave the needy appears in the Law of Moses. Hence the
Exodus 22:25; Law's inflexible prohibitions upon all practices of usury
Leviticus 25: 36-37; within the community of the children of Israel, and hence
Deuteronomy 23:19-20 the ancient Jewish condemnation of fiduciary interest.
Psalm 15[14]:5; Hence also the care extended in the Law to ensure that
Ezekiel 18:17 neither Israelites *nor their neighbors* be reduced to a state
Exodus 12:49; 22:21- of absolute impoverishment. Moreover, the Law not only
22; Leviticus 19:9-10; prohibited interest on loans, but mandated that every sev-
23:22; 25:35-38; enth year should be a Sabbatical, a *shmita*, a fallow year,
Deuteronomy 15:1-11 during which debts between Israelites were to be remit-
ted; and then went even further in imposing the Sabbath
of Sabbath-Years, the Year of Jubilee, in which all debts
were excused. In this way, the difference between creditors and debtors could be for a time erased, and a kind of
equitable balance restored. And the unremitting denun-
ciation of those who exploit the poor or ignore their plight

is a persistent theme running through the proclamations of the prophets of Israel. It is not by accident, moreover, that Christ's parables and injunctions so often advert to the crushing weight of indebtedness under which the poorer classes of his day struggled; and modern Christians should not allow an overly spiritualized reading of his language to hide the social issues he was addressing from view. It is just such debt, mercilessly exacted from those who had fallen victim to interest charges too exorbitant to meet, that Christ referred to as *the Mammon of injustice* and that both Jewish and Christian tradition condemn as usury. When Christ spoke of the law courts of his day, he was speaking of what was preponderantly a legal mechanism by which creditors, on the pretext of debts engineered to be beyond all possible discharge, could despoil their debtors of all their material goods. It is just such creditors that the Letter of James denounces, and it is almost certainly just such debts from which the Lord's Prayer—in its original context—petitions for relief, just such trials into which it asks God not to lead us, and just such a creditor (*the evil man*) from whom it begs rescue. To this day, however, there is scarcely any area of public policy, even in the most developed of countries, where abuses of credit and debt are controlled by rational and humane regulation. The poor of most societies are victims of unprincipled credit institutions, and as a rule enjoy little protection from creditors who have exploited their need to place them in a condition of perpetual debt. If the Church truly desires to encourage social practices that reflect the love, mercy, and justice of God as revealed in Christ, it must certainly be willing to protest laws that

Isaiah 3:13-15; 5:8; 10:1-2; Jeremiah 5:27-28: Amos 4:1; etc.

Luke 16:9

cf. Luke 12:58-59

James 2:6

Matthew 6:9-13

do not protect the vulnerable against unscrupulous and rapacious creditors, and that do not provide compassionate public alternatives to unregulated or inadequately regulated private creditors for those who need to alleviate their privations and supply their needs. Moreover, the Church must recall that the mechanisms of indebtedness function to impoverish nations as much as individuals, and that a cruel inflexibility on the part of creditor nations toward debtor nations is often the cause of immense human misery, thwarting every hope of economic development and social advancement among disadvantaged peoples. Christ instructed his followers to forgive their debtors, and Christ's Church can do no other than tirelessly to advocate the forgiveness of international debt by wealthier nations.

§40   The Church has a special vocation to recall that, with the exception of unrelieved hunger, there is no crueler deprivation endured by the poor throughout the world than lack of access to decent medical care. Christ, again, brought his good tidings not only to the destitute, but to the lame, the blind, the disabled, the sick, and the suffering. His ministry was marked by no more radiant sign of God's liberating love for his creatures than his power of healing, which he offered freely to all who sought relief from their physical and spiritual afflictions. Christ indeed numbered visitation of the sick among the necessary criteria of salvation. A Church that strives to proclaim that *Matthew 25:31-46* same love to all nations, and to demand of every society the justice that God requires of all human beings, must insist that every government seek, by whatever powers and resources it has at its disposal, to provide universal healthcare, of as high a quality as possible, for all its citizens. That those who cannot procure such care for themselves should be given access to it, by public policy and at the public expense, and that such care should not leave the needy at the mercy of insurance agencies that exact huge premiums while supplying meager benefits, and that the poor should not be further impoverished in exchange for the privilege of living and thriving among their fellow citizens, is the absolute *minimum* that the Church should expect of countries with developed economies. Nor can such obligations end at national borders. Richer nations are morally obliged, from a Christian point of view, to seek to improve medical conditions for persons everywhere, to the degree that they can. Often this means seeking to provide affordable pharmaceuticals in countries whose citizens cannot bear the costs of the most effective and current medical treatments for serious ailments. Often it will entail direct assistance from physicians and other medical professionals. Whatever it involves, however, the Orthodox Church is bound to call for and participate in the ceaseless effort to bring healing to all peoples in the name of Christ, the healer of souls and bodies.

§41   In any nation, the poor are almost always the first to suffer as a result of any general adverse conditions, natural or social, economic or political. And, in many places, poverty is as much the result of racial or class discrimination as of mere personal misfortune. The current environmental crisis, for instance—anthropogenic climate change, toxic pollution of water sources and soils around the world, ubiquitous damage to the entire ecosystem by microplastics and other contaminants, deforestation, soil erosion, the rapid decline of biological diversity, and so forth—is an incalculable catastrophe for the entire planet and for all terrestrial life. Almost invariably, however, the greatest immediate burden falls upon the less economically developed quarters of the earth, where governments can do—or elect to do—very little to protect the destitute against the consequences of industrial waste and general ecological devastation. It is the poor, moreover, who are most regularly displaced and further impoverished by the destruction of the environment around them. And, even in nations of the developed world, it tends to be the poorest citizens who are most routinely exposed to the dire results of environmental degradation and who lack the resources to remedy their situations. So long as immense discrepancies in wealth exist between nations and between individuals, social and political power will be the possession primarily of the rich, as will whatever degree of relative immunity from the consequences of human folly and corruption or natural calamity can be achieved by material means. So too will the best avenues of education or professional advancement, the best healthcare, the best legal protections, the best financial opportunities, the best access to institutions of political power, and so on. Great economic inequality is, inevitably, social injustice; it is, moreover, according to the teachings of Christ, a thing abominable in the eyes of God. Whole schools of economics arose in the twentieth century at the service of such inequality, arguing that it is a necessary concomitant of any functioning economy. Without fail, however, the arguments employed by these schools are tautologous at best, and proof of how impoverished the human moral imagination can make itself in servitude to ideology. The Church must trust instead in the assurances of Christ that, for those who seek God's Kingdom and its justice, God will provide all things. It must always, as heir to the missions of the prophets and to the Gospel of the incarnate God, be a voice first for the poor, and a voice raised whenever necessary against the rich and powerful, and against governments that neglect or abuse the weak in order to serve the interests of the strong. And the Church must in every generation, remembering the example of the Church of the Apostolic age, ask of every society whether there are not effective means—and perhaps new economic models—by which it would be possible to achieve a more just distribution of wealth, and thereby a more radical commitment to the common good, of society and of the planet we all must share. For St. Maria Skobstova, this is a mandate addressed to everyone seeking to rise from earth to heaven and rejoice with the angels when a cup of water is offered to a single individual in the name of the Lord:

> A person should have a more attentive attitude to his brother's flesh than to his own. Christian love teaches us to give our brother not only material but also spiritual gifts. We must give him our last shirt and our last crust of bread. Here personal charity is as necessary and justified as the broadest social work. In this sense there is no doubt that the Christian is called to social work. He is called to organize a better life for the workers, to provide for the old, to build hospitals, care for children, fight against exploitation, injustice, want, lawlessness.[37]

---

37   Maria Skobtsova, "The Second Gospel Commandment," *Mother Maria*

V. WAR, PEACE, AND VIOLENCE

For the peace of the whole world . . .

§42 The beauty and goodness of creation declare themselves lavishly in the very frame of nature; but ours is a fallen world as well, enslaved to death, disfigured everywhere by violence, cruelty, ignorance, and strife. The violence of nature is already a sign of a created order corrupted by alienation from God; but the violence intentionally perpetrated by rational human agents, especially when organized and prosecuted on a massive scale as war between peoples or nations, is the most terrible manifestation of the reign of sin and death in all things. Nothing is more contrary to God's will for creatures fashioned in his image and likeness than violence one against another, and nothing more sacrilegious than the organized practice of mass killing. All human violence is in some sense rebellion against God and the divinely created order. As Gideon proclaimed, *the Lord is peace*; and as St. Silouan the Athonite affirms, "our brother is our life."[38] So it is that the Church proclaims with the Psalmist: *How very good and pleasant it is when kindred live together in unity!* The opening chapters of Genesis tell us that harmony, peace, communion, and abundance are the true "grammar" of creation as God has uttered it in his eternal Word. And yet all peoples live according to a law of aggression instead, at times tacit, at times explicit. And, while the affliction of war has been a constant fact of human experience throughout history, the modern age of the nation state and the late modern development of

Judges 6:24

Psalm 133[132]:1

Skobtsova: Essential Writings, 54.

38   *St. Silouan the Athonite*, 47.

technologies of destruction of hitherto unimagined power have transformed what was once merely the tragically
perennial condition of human society into an acute crisis
for the entire species.

$43   Violence is the intentional use of physical, psychologi-
cal, fiscal, or social force against others or against oneself,
causing harm, misery, or death. Its forms and manifesta-
tions are too numerous to calculate. They include physical
assault of every kind, sexual assault, domestic violence,
abortion, hate-crimes, acts of terrorism, acts of war, and
so forth, as well as acts of self-mutilation and suicide. All
these result in damage to all parties involved: physical,
mental, and spiritual damage to the victims of violence,
but also to its perpetrators. In fact, research confirms that
the effect of violence almost invariably extends beyond
the parties immediately involved, and works its harm—
even if only subtly—on all of humanity and all of creation.
Like a contagion, violence's effects spread throughout the
"total Adam" and the whole world, often rendering love
difficult or even impossible by corrupting human imagi-
nations and severing the fragile bonds of love and trust
that bind persons together in community. Every act of violence against another human being is, in truth, violence
against a member of one's own family, and the killing of
another human being—even when and where inevitable—is the killing of one's own brother or sister. To the degree that our lives are sustained or protected or enriched
by violence, moreover—even if prosecuted by the state
on our behalf without our awareness—we are to some
degree complicit in the sin of Cain. In the end, we may
justly say that violence is sin *par excellence*. It is the perfect

contradiction of our created nature and our supernatural vocation to seek union in love with God and our neighbor. It is the negation of the divine order of reality, which is one of peace, communion, and charity. It is the denial and suppression of the divine dignity inherent in every soul, and an assault upon the image of God in each of us.

$44   The Orthodox Church cannot, naturally, approve of violence, either as an end in itself or even as a means for achieving some other end, whether this be in the form of physical violence, sexual abuse, or the abuse of authority. In every celebration of the Eucharist, the Church prays in her Great Litany "for the peace of the whole world, let us pray to the Lord." Peace, for the Church, is more than a state of armistice lightly imposed upon a naturally violent world. It is, rather, a real revelation of the still deeper reality of creation as God intends it, and as God fashioned it in his eternal counsels. It is the restoration of creation to its true form, if only in part. True peace is the very presence of God among us. A great many saints of the Church, such as St. Moses the Ethiopian and St. Seraphim of Sarov, have freely chosen to suffer violence without reciprocating it or seeking redress. According to sacred tradition, the saintly Kievan princes Boris and Gleb offered up both their kingdoms and their lives rather than lift their hands in violence against others to defend themselves or their possessions. The Church honors all such martyrs for peace as witnesses to the power of love, to the goodness of creation in its first and final forms, and to the ideal of human conduct established by Christ during his earthly ministry.

$45   And yet the Church knows that it cannot foresee every contingency to which persons or peoples must respond at any given moment, and that in a fallen and broken world there are times when there is no perfectly peaceful means of cultivating peace for everyone. While unequivocally condemning violence of any kind, it nevertheless recognizes the tragic necessity of individuals or communities or states using force to defend themselves and others from the immediate threat of violence. Thus the child facing an abusive family member, the woman facing a violent husband, the law-abiding citizen facing a violent attacker, the bystander witnessing an assault, and the community or nation under attack by a cruel aggressor may decide, in a manner consistent with their faith and with love, to defend themselves and their neighbor against the perpetrators of violence. Self-defense without spite may be excusable; and defense of the oppressed against their oppressors is often a moral obligation; but at times, tragically, neither can be accomplished without the judicious use of force. In such cases, prayer and discernment are necessary, as is the sincere effort to bring about reconciliation, forgiveness, and healing. The Orthodox Church, moreover, recognizes and affirms the responsibility of legitimate government to protect the vulnerable, to prevent and limit violence, and to promote peace among persons and between peoples. Thus in the litanies recited in its divine services it prays fervently "for civil authorities, that they may govern in peace." One of the primary purposes of any government is defense of the lives and welfare of those who shelter under its protection. But government achieves this best when working to reduce violence and to encourage peaceful coexistence, precisely by seeking to institute just and compassionate laws and to grant equal protection and liberty to all the communities over which it may exercise power, including ethnic or religious minorities. The use of force must always be the last resort of any just government, and must never become excessive.

$46   The Orthodox Church has not historically insisted upon a strictly pacifist response to war, violence, and oppression; neither has the Church prohibited the faithful from serving in the military or police. Its military saints, often martyrs of the Church, are a case in point. And yet the Orthodox Church has also never developed any kind of "Just War Theory" that seeks in advance, and under a set of abstract principles, to justify and morally endorse a state's use of violence when a set of general criteria are met. Indeed, it could never refer to war as "holy" or "just." Instead, the Church has merely recognized the inescapably tragic reality that sin sometimes requires a heartbreaking choice between allowing violence to continue or employing force to bring that violence to an end, even though it never ceases to pray for peace, and even though it knows that the use of coercive force is always a morally imperfect response to any situation. That said, no one—even if conscripted under arms—is morally required to participate in actions that he or it knows to be contrary to justice and to the precepts of the Gospel. Christian conscience must always reign supreme over the imperatives of national interest. Above all, a Christian must remain ever mindful that things that would be considered acts of terrorism when perpetrated by individuals or organized factions—the random murder of innocent civilians, for instance, for the sake of advancing a political cause—do not become morally acceptable when they are perpetrated instead by recognized states, or when they are achieved with the use of advanced military technology. Indeed, it is arguable that one of the defining features of modern warfare is the effective conflation of the strategies of battle and the intentional terrorization of civilian populations.

$47   The Church's teachings, which always aim at our salvation and flourishing in Christ, and her prayers, which request "that which is good and beneficial to our souls, and peace in the world," should remind us of the spiritual effects and dangers of war and violence, even for those who have no choice but to defend themselves and their neighbors by force. As Christ teaches us, *no one has greater love than this, to lay down one's life for one's friends.* This is a *John 15:13* proclamation that directs our gaze first to the cross of Christ, which was a place primarily of surrender to violence and the refusal of retribution. As such, the cross is not in itself any kind of justification for the use of force in defense of oneself or others. It does, however, remind us that, when one must defend the innocent against the rapacious, the only proper Christian motivation for doing so is love. The Church rejects all violence—including defensive acts—that are prompted by hate, racism, revenge, selfishness, economic exploitation, nationalism, or personal glory. Such motives, which are all too often the hidden springs behind the waging of so-called "just wars," are never blessed by God. Moreover, even in those rare situations in which the use of force is not absolutely prohibited, the Orthodox Church still discerns a need for spiritual and emotional healing among all persons involved. Whether one suffers or inflicts violence, no matter what the cause, the whole person is always harmed, and this harm is invariably deleterious to one's relationship with God, neighbor, and creation. Hence, for example, St. Basil recommended that a soldier who kills in the course of fighting in a defensive war, though not himself an intentional "murderer," should nonetheless abstain from the Eucharist for a limited time, and undertake penitential discipline, as his "hands are not clean."[39] Many victims of assault, but also many soldiers, police officers, and perpetrators of violence, find the experience spiritually devastating, and in consequence find their capacity for faith, hope, and love deeply damaged. The Church suffers with all such persons, praying for the healing and salvation of all who are "sick, suffering, and in captivity" (Divine Liturgy of St. John Chrysostom). In all cases, the Orthodox Church must never cease to offer ministries of spiritual healing to those who have been the victims of violence and to those who have used violence, offering care to all who are receptive to God's mercy and grace. Christ's own suffering, crucifixion, and resurrection teach us that God's love is able to enter fully into the abyss of sin and death and overcome them, turning even the cross, the worst imaginable instrument of intolerable fear and violent death, into a "weapon of peace" and a "life-giving tree" (From the Feast of the Exaltation of the Cross).

§48   The Orthodox Church rejects capital punishment, and does so out of faithfulness to the Gospel and to the example of the Apostolic Church. It upholds the laws of forgiveness and reconciliation as the chief imperatives of Christian culture, while ever pointing to the potential and promise of transformation in Christ. The Church

---

39   Basil, Canon 13. See his *Letter* 188. PG 32.681C.

insists upon the responsibility of all governments to limit
violence in every way that they can. Inasmuch as capital
punishment returns evil for evil, it cannot be considered
a virtuous or even tolerable practice. While some might
seek to justify the death penalty as an expression of pro-
portional justice, Christians may not adopt such a logic.
In the Gospels, Christ repeatedly rejects the very principle
of proportionality. He requires of his followers a rule of
forgiveness that not only exceeds the demands of "natural" justice, but that even sets the wrath of the law aside in
favor of its own much deeper logic of mercy (as in the case
of the woman taken in adultery). And the New Testament
as a whole consistently demands of Christians that they
exercise limitless forgiveness. Occasionally the words of
Paul in Romans 13:1–7 (where he alludes to *the bearers of
the short-sword*, the *machairophoroi*, possessed of police
authority) are invoked as supporting the death penalty,
but there is no reason to suppose Paul had the practice of
capital punishment in mind in writing those verses; and,
even if he had, those verses do not give any instructions
on the Christian view of just governance, but rather merely set a standard of peaceful Christian conduct under the
pagan government of the first century. It is simply a fact
of history that the more or less ubiquitous conviction of
the earliest Christians—those whose communities most
immediately arose from the Church of the Apostles—was
that Christ's command not to judge others was more than
a mere prohibition of private prejudice. Hence Christians
were not supposed to serve as magistrates or soldiers,
chiefly because these professions required one, respective-
ly, to sentence persons to death or to carry out executions.

This refusal to participate in the civic machinery of juris-
prudential violence was one of the most distinctive marks
of the early Christian movement, and an object of scorn
on the part of pagan observers. The witness of the earliest
Christian writers of the post-apostolic age confirms this.
St. Justin Martyr asserted that a Christian would rather
die than take a life, even in the case of a legal sentence of
death.[40] According to the *The Apostolic Tradition*, traditionally attributed to Hippolytus of Rome, no one intending to
become a soldier could be received into the Church, while
those who were already under arms at the time of their
conversion were forbidden to carry out even a properly
pronounced order of execution.[41] Arnobius clearly stated
that Christians were not allowed to impose the death
penalty at all, even when it was perfectly just. Athenagoras stated that the killing even of those guilty of capital
offenses must be repugnant to Christians, as they are
obliged to view all killing of humans as a pollution of the
soul.[42] Minucius Felix, St. Cyprian, and Tertullian all took
it for granted that, for Christians, the innocent may never
slay the guilty. According to Lactantius, a Christian could
neither kill a justly condemned criminal nor even arraign
another person for a capital crime.[43] It is true that, after
the conversion of the empire, the Church had to accept the
reality of an established system of jurisprudence and cor-
rection that included capital punishment, a system that
it could ameliorate only to a degree. Even so, the greatest

---

40   Justin, *First Apology* 39. PG 6.388B.

41   *The Apostolic Tradition* 16.9. See *The Apostolic Tradition: A Commentary*,
Minneapolis, MN: Fortress Press, 2002.

42   Athenagoras, *A Plea for the Christians* 35. PG 6.968C.

43   Lactantius, *Divine Institutes* 6.20. PL 6.705B.

of the Church Fathers consistently argued against the full application of the law in capital cases, in part because capital punishment constitutes a usurpation of God's role as just judge, and in part because it obviates the criminal's opportunity for repentance. And, as St. John Chrysostom asked in the course of praising the emperor for refraining from the "legal slaughter" of rioters: "If you slay God's image, how can you then revoke the deed?"[44] The prevailing view among the Fathers was essentially that the Sermon on the Mount's prohibitions of retaliation sets the standard for Christians in both the private and the public spheres, for on the cross Christ at once perfected the refusal of violence and exhausted the law's wrath. As the centuries wore on, admittedly, and as the Church accommodated itself to the cultures and rulers with which it allied itself, this prophetic hostility to capital punishment was frequently forgotten, and for long periods; but it remains the ideal of the New Testament and of the Church in its earliest dawn, and in our day it is possible to recover that ideal fully and state it anew without hesitation. Thus, while the Church fully recognizes that the state is obliged to imprison those who might cause harm to others, it calls for the abolition of the death penalty in all countries. The Church appeals also to the consciences of persons everywhere, and asks them to recognize that capital punishment is almost invariably a penalty reserved for those who lack the resources to afford the best legal defense or who belong to racial or religious minorities.

§49   For Orthodox Christians, the way of peace, of dialogue and diplomacy, of forgiveness and reconciliation is always

---

44   John Chrysostom, *Homily on the Statues* 17.1. PG 49.173B.

preferable to the use of violence, capital punishment, or police or military force. The highest expression of Christian holiness in response to violence is perhaps found in those who strive every day to create understanding and respect among persons, to prevent conflict, to reunite those who are divided, to seek to create economic and social mechanisms for alleviating the problems that often lead to violence, and to welcome and care for those who are marginalized and suffering. It is found among those who dedicate themselves to extirpating the spiritual roots of violence in themselves and others. For this reason, our Lord proclaims: *Blessed are the peacemakers, for they shall be* *Matthew 5:9* *called children of God.* As we pray, "Our Father," we accept our calling as "children of God" to be peacemakers within our families and local communities, to work diligently to prevent violence and war from arising, and to heal the brokenness that persists below the surface, in ourselves and others. As St. Basil says, "without peace with all people, in as far as it is within my possibilities, I cannot call myself a worthy servant of Jesus Christ."[45] And, as he also adds, "nothing is so characteristic of a Christian as to be a peacemaker."[46]

VI. ECUMENICAL RELATIONS
AND RELATIONS WITH OTHER FAITHS

Let us pray for the unity of all

$50   The Orthodox Church understands itself to be the one, holy, catholic, and apostolic Church, of which the Nicene-Constantinopolitan symbol speaks. It is the Church of the

---

45   Basil, *Epistle* 203, 2. PG 32.737B.
46   Basil, *Epistle* 114. PG 32.528B.

Councils, continuous in charism and commission from the time of the Apostolic Council in Jerusalem up to the present day.[47] It lacks nothing essential to the full catholicity and full unity of the body of Christ, and possesses the fullness of all sacramental, magisterial, and pastoral grace. As Fr. Georges Florovsky wrote:

Acts 15.5–29

> The Orthodox are bound to claim that the only 'specific' or 'distinctive' feature about their own position in 'divided Christendom' is the fact that the Orthodox Church is essentially identical with the Church of all ages, and indeed with the 'Early Church.' In other words, she is not *a* Church, but *the* Church. It is a formidable, but a fair and a just claim. There is here more than just an unbroken *historic continuity*, which is indeed quite obvious. There is above all an ultimate *spiritual and ontological identity*, the same faith, the same spirit, the same ethos. And this constitutes the distinctive mark of Orthodoxy. 'This is the Apostolic faith, this is the faith of the Fathers, this is the Orthodox faith, this faith has established the universe.'[48]

$51   That said, the Orthodox Church earnestly seeks unity with all Christians out of love and desire to share the spiritual riches of its tradition with all who seek the face of Christ. Moreover, it understands that the particular cultural forms of tradition must not be confused with either the true apostolic authority or the sacramental grace with which it has been entrusted. The Church seeks sustained dialogue with Christians of other communions in

47   Holy and Great Council, Encyclical, §2.
48   Georges Florovsky, "The Ethos of the Orthodox Church," *The Ecumenical Review* 12.2 (1960), 183–198 [at 186].

order to offer them a full understanding of the beauty of Orthodoxy, not in order to convert them to some cultural "Byzantinism." It does so also in order to learn from the experiences of Christians throughout the world, to understand the many cultural expressions of Christianity, and to seek unity among all who call upon the name of Jesus. Orthodoxy cannot be silent and must reach out and call all Christians to the fullness of the faith:

> The Orthodox Church has the mission and duty to transmit and preach all the truth contained in Holy Scripture and Holy Tradition, which also bestows upon the Church her catholic character. The responsibility of the Orthodox Church for unity as well as her ecumenical mission were articulated by the Ecumenical Councils. These stressed most especially the indissoluble bond between true faith and sacramental communion.[49]

§52   Though visible sacramental unity among all Christians is at present only a remote hope, nothing lies beyond the power of God's Spirit, and the Church cannot relent in her labors to achieve a final reunion of all who come together in Christ's name. Until that day, so long as their hearts and minds are open to the promptings of God's Word and Spirit, Christians of all communions can meet together in love and work together for the transformation of the world. In particular, they can cooperate with one another in works of charity, thereby making God's love manifest to the world, and in efforts to advance social and civil justice, thereby proclaiming God's righteousness and peace to all peoples. Moreover, even if they cannot as yet enjoy perfect

---

49   Holy and Great Council, Relations of the Orthodox Church with the Rest of the Christian World, §2-3.

communion in the full sacramental life of the Church, all Christians are called by their baptism in the Holy Trinity to gather together in prayer, to repent of past misunderstandings and offences against their brothers and sisters, and to love one another as fellow servants and heirs of the Kingdom of God. *By this, all shall know that you are my disciples: if you have love for one another.*   John 13:35

§53   The Orthodox Church enjoys especially close relations with those communions that are directly descended from the ancient Apostolic Church and that share something like her understanding of the apostolic charism of episcopal succession and something like her sacramental theology: the ancient churches of Egypt and Ethiopia, of Armenia, of the Assyrian tradition, of Canterbury, and of Rome. Thus, the Church has important bilateral dialogues with the Roman Catholic Church and the Anglican Communion, and it prays that these dialogues may bear fruit in a complete unity with the Church. But all Christian communions are her kin and her love for all is equally unqualified. For more than a century, then, the Orthodox Church has played a leading role in the movement towards Christian unity, out of obedience to our Lord's supplication and exhortation *that all may be one.* The Ecumenical Patriarch-   John 17:21 ate, in particular, has been at the forefront of the Orthodox engagement with Christians of other communions, and has remained a steadfast participant in numerous bilateral and multi-lateral dialogues with other major Christian churches. The Ecumenical Patriarchate was, in fact, one of the founding members of the World Council of Churches, and has continuously maintained an official representative presence at that council's central offices.

§54   In short, the Church is dedicated to a sustained dialogue with other Christians. Dialogue, in the Orthodox understanding, is essentially and primordially a reflection of the dialogue between God and humanity: it is initiated by God and conducted through the divine Logos (*dia-logos*), our Lord and Savior Jesus Christ. Pervading all human life, dialogue takes place in all our encounters, personal, social, or political, and must always be extended to those who adhere to religions different from ours. And in all our connections and relationships, the Word of God is mystically present, ever guiding our exchange of words and ideas towards a spiritual union of hearts in him. Naturally, the Orthodox Church considers itself responsible always to interpret other traditions and perspectives in terms of what was revealed to it by God. In so doing, it is open to *whatever is true, whatever is honorable,* *Philippians 4:8* *whatever is pleasing, whatever is commendable,* and is ready to rejoice whenever it discovers these in her partners of dialogue. Our commitment to ecumenical relations with other Christian confessions reflects this openness to all who sincerely seek the truth as the incarnate Logos, Jesus Christ, and who remain true to their conscience, even while we continue to bear witness to the fullness of the Christian faith in the Orthodox Church. Moreover, the Church can stand with other Christians in this way not only out of solidarity in light of a shared history and moral vision, but also because such Christian groups, through their Trinitarian baptism and confession of the faith of the Councils, profess and share many aspects of Orthodox teaching and tradition.

§55   God is Father of all the families of the heavens and the earth. God's Logos pervades all things, and all things were created through his Logos. God's Spirit is everywhere, enlightening and enlivening all of reality. Thus creation universally declares the power, wisdom, and grace of its maker, while at all times and in all places God is present to those who seek the truth. The Orthodox Church exists as the concrete reality of Christ's mystical body in time, always bearing witness to *the light of the knowledge of the glory of God in the face of Christ.* It is for this reason that the *2 Corinthians 4:6* Church not only reaches out and witnesses to Orthodoxy to various Christian confessions, with whom the Orthodox Church enjoys historic dialogue, but also reaches outward to meet non-Christian religions and faith communities that are open to the truth and the call of God. In this regard, it also affirms, and has done so since the earliest centuries of the faith, that God's Logos shines forth in the whole frame of the created world and speaks to all hearts in the still small voice of conscience, and that wherever truth is revered the Spirit of God is at work. St. Justin Martyr, for instance, declared that knowledge of God's Logos had been imparted by God not only to the children of Israel, but to the Greek philosophers who had never known Christ, and to all peoples, inasmuch as seeds of the eternal Logos have been planted in all human beings; thus, he says, all who have lived in harmony with this Logos are already in some sense Christians, while Christians may claim as their own any and every truth known to the nations of the earth by God's inspiration.[50] According to St.

---

50   Justin, *First Apology* 46. PG6.397B. And *Second Apology* 8, 10, and 13. PG 6.457A, 460B, and 465B.

Maximus the Confessor, the primordial *logoi* underlying
and indwelling all things reside in the one Logos of God,
and find their historical center in Christ.[51] The Church
knows, moreover, that the full mystery of God's Logos
transcends human comprehension, and communicates
itself in ways too numerous and wonderful to calculate or
conceive. The Church thus seeks dialogue with other religious traditions not out of any desire to alter the deposit
of its faith, much less out of any anxiety regarding that
deposit's sufficiency, but out of a reverent love for all who
seek God and his goodness, and in a firm certitude that
God has left no people without a share in the knowledge
of his glory and grace. This is not to deny, of course, that
there are many irreconcilable differences between the
Church's understanding of the truth and that of other religious traditions, and it certainly has no desire to obscure
this reality. It seeks neither to make compromises regarding her own essential beliefs nor condescendingly to treat
those of other faiths as inconsequential. At the same time,
knowing that God reveals himself in countless ways and
with boundless inventiveness, the Church enters into dialogue with other faiths prepared to be amazed and de-
lighted by the variety and beauty of God's generous mani-
festations of divine goodness, grace, and wisdom among
all peoples.

§56   Though the Orthodox Church seeks deeper bonds of
amity with all faiths, it recognizes her unique responsibility with regard to the other two "peoples of the book," the
Abrahamic traditions of Islam and Judaism, with which
it has longstanding dialogues and alongside which it has

---

51   Maximus, *Ambiguum* 7. PG 91.1081C. See *On Difficulties in the Church Fathers*, vol. 1, 75–141.

lived for millennia. Therefore, the Church can and does engage the beauty and spiritual truths of Islam in all its multiple traditions, acknowledging points of contact with it especially in its affirmation of the Virgin Birth[52] and its recognition of Jesus as the Messiah, Messenger, Word, and Spirit of God.[53] Although Orthodoxy cannot agree with Islam in its rejection of the Incarnation and of God as Trinity, it is nevertheless able to pursue meaningful dialogue with all parts of the Islamic Ummah regarding the proper understanding of these central Christian teachings. It believes that the common roots of Christianity and Islam in the Middle East, the common affirmation of the message of the unity of God, as well as the common recognition of the holiness and truth of God's Word and his Prophets, the importance of prayer and ascesis, as well as the struggle to discern the will of God in all things, invite Islam and Orthodoxy to enter into an intimate conversation for the advancement of peace and understanding among all peoples.

§57   As to Judaism, when the eternal Son of God became human he became incarnate as a Jew, born within the body of Israel, an heir to God's covenants with his chosen people. He came in fulfillment of God's saving promises to his people, as the Messiah of Israel. The first blood he shed for the redemption of the world was exacted on the day of his circumcision; his first confession before the world concerning the justice of God was in the synagogue, as was the first declaration of his mission to the world; his *Luke 4:18–21* ministry resumed the language of the great prophets of

---

52   *Quran* 3:47, 19:16-21, 21:91.

53   *Quran* 4:171.

Israel; and he was executed by a pagan authority under the title "King of the Jews." It was to Israel that God declared himself as The One Who Is, to Israel that God gave the Law as a language of love and communion, with Israel that God established an everlasting covenant, and to Israel that he proclaimed, *I will bless those who bless you and curse those who curse you, and in you shall all the families of the* *Genesis 12:3* *earth be blessed.* As the Apostle Paul emphasized, Christians are saved in Christ only in being grafted like wild olive branches into the cultivated olive tree of Israel, and the branches do not support—but rather are supported by— *Romans 11:16–24* the root. Orthodox Christians look to the Jewish communities throughout the world not merely as to practitioners of another creed, but as to, in some sense, their spiritual elders in the history of God's saving revelations, and as to the guardians of that precious inheritance that is the first full manifestation of God's saving presence in history. It is, sadly, necessary to state these things with a special emphasis at this moment. In recent years, we have witnessed a revival in many quarters of the Western world of the most insidious ideologies of national, religious, and even racial identity in general, and of anti-Semitic movements in particular. Bigotry and violence against Jews have long been a conspicuous evil of the cultures of Christendom; the greatest systematic campaign of mass murder and attempted genocide in European history was undertaken against the Jews of Europe; and—while some Orthodox clergy and laity demonstrated exceptional generosity and even sacrificial compassion to their Jewish brothers and sisters, earning from them the honorific "righteous among the nations"—other historically Orthodox nations have dark histories of anti-Semitic violence and oppression. For all these evils, Christians must seek God's forgiveness. In expiation for those crimes against the Jewish people specifically committed in Orthodox lands, the Church seeks both God's forgiveness as well as a deeper relation of love and regard with Jewish communities and the Jewish faith.

§58   The story of other non-Orthodox Christian religious traditions is not yet finished, and Orthodoxy affirms that like other non-Orthodox Christian bodies they only find their coherence and clarity within the Orthodox Church. As for other religions, the Orthodox Church takes encouragement from the words of the Apostle Paul to the Athenians at the Areopagus: *What therefore you worship as unknown, this I proclaim to you.* From this the Church   Acts 17:23 is given license to proclaim that the true God in whom all humanity lives and moves and has its being is worshipped by peoples everywhere, Christian and non-Christian alike. And this makes it only more eager to make all persons and peoples aware that the face of this one true God shines forth unobscured in the face of Jesus Christ. Moreover, the Church—illumined by that radiance—enters into dialogue with other faiths fully prepared to be instructed by many of their own speculative, cultural, and spiritual achievements. It may be that, just as the Church of the early centuries profited from and in time baptized many of the philosophical, religious, and cultural riches of pre-Christian Europe, Asia Minor, and the Near East, so too may it now discover new ways of articulating the deposit of faith or new ways of thinking about its cultural expressions and conceptual forms by exposure to, say, the

great philosophies and faiths of India, or to the traditions
of China and the greater Far East, or to the spiritual experiences of tribal peoples throughout the world, and so on.
Again, as Justin Martyr insisted, whatsoever is true and
godly is welcome to us, for the Logos is everywhere and
shines forth in all places.

§59   The Orthodox Church seeks, moreover, to make common cause with all persons and peoples who cultivate and
guard the things of the spirit over against the corrosive
materialisms of the modern age, and with all who share
her abhorrence of those forms of religious extremism and
fundamentalism that blasphemously associate their ha-
treds, bigotries, and violences with the name of God. The
Encyclical of the Holy and Great Council states that,

> honest interfaith dialogue contributes to the devel-
> opment of mutual trust and to the promotion of
> peace and reconciliation. The Church strives to make
> 'the peace from on high' more tangibly felt on earth.
> True peace is not achieved by force of arms, but only
> through love that *does not seek its own*. The oil of faith
> must be used to soothe and heal the wounds of oth-
> ers, not to rekindle new fires of hatred.[54]

1 Corinthians 13:5

For this reason, the Orthodox Church approaches interreligious dialogue in full recognition of the real differences between traditions, but firmly insists nonetheless
on the real possibility of peaceful coexistence and cooperation among different faiths. Above all, it seeks to overcome ignorance, hostility, and fear with reciprocal comprehension and the peace of true friendship.

For Orthodox Christians living in non-Orthodox coun-   §60
tries, interreligious encounters and dialogue are and will

---

54   Paragraph 17.

continue to be important means through which respect for religious differences and proclamation of the truth are realized. Interreligious dialogue is not merely about finding common ground or identifying areas of commonality; it is also an encounter with others on a personal and human level. It requires respect for the human person, created in God's image, and for God's love of all humanity and all creation. Encounter and dialogue require risk at the level both of the person as well as of the community. All dialogue is personal, then, since it involves the interaction of unique, irreplaceable persons, Christian or not, whose personhood is intricately connected to their individual, social, cultural, and religious histories. All dialogue is a communal undertaking, however, since fundamental to Orthodox ecclesiology is the notion that the individual member of the Church exists only in communion or relation with the whole body of the Church and ultimately with Christ, who is the head of the Church.

VII. ORTHODOXY AND HUMAN RIGHTS

You have created us in your image and likeness

$61   It is not by chance that the language of human rights, as well as legal conventions and institutions devised to protect and advance those rights, notably arose in nations whose moral cultures had been formed by Christian beliefs. Today, we employ the concept of innate human rights as a kind of neutral grammar by which to negotiate civil and legal mechanisms for the preservation of human dignity, general liberty, social stability, equal rights for all, complete political enfranchisement, economic justice, and equality before the law, as well as the institution of international conventions for the protection of the rights of minorities, migrants, and asylum-seekers, and against war crimes and crimes against humanity. But the historical roots of such ideas reach down deep into the soil of the Gospel and its proclamation—in the midst of an imperial culture to which such ideas were largely alien—of the infinite value of every soul, and of the full personal dignity of every individual. Every significant modern statement and charter of universal civil rights, from the French Assembly's *Déclaration des droits de l'homme et du citoyen* (1789) to the United Nations' *Universal Declaration of Human Rights* (1948) and its sequels, has confidently asserted that the moral claims of every human being upon his or her society and its laws are more original and more inviolable than the rights of estates or governments or institutions of power. This is an assurance largely inherited from the Jewish and Christian sources of European civilization. Orthodox Christians, then, may and should happily adopt the language of human rights when seeking to promote justice and peace among peoples and nations, and when seeking to defend the weak against the powerful, the oppressed against their oppressors, and the indigent against those who seek to exploit them. The language of human rights may not say all that can and should be said about the profound dignity and glory of creatures fashioned after the image and likeness of God; but it is a language that honors that reality in a way that permits international and interfaith cooperation in the work of civil rights and civil justice, and that therefore says much that should be said. The Orthodox Church, therefore, lends its voice to the call to protect and advance human rights everywhere, and to recognize those rights as both fundamental to and inalienable from every single human life.

$62   God created humankind after his own image and likeness, and has endowed every man, woman, and child with the full spiritual dignity of persons fashioned in conformity with the divine personhood of the Father, Son, and Holy Spirit. In so doing, he brought into being a new sphere of created freedom, the distinctly human space of liberty. According to Orthodox tradition, humanity occupies a peculiarly mediatorial role in creation, existing at once in the realms of matter and spirit, comprehensively possessing the characteristics of both, and constituting a unity between them. As such, humanity is the priestly presence of spiritual freedom within the world of material causality and organic process, imparting the light of rational freedom to all of the material cosmos, and offering up the life of the world to God. And the Church has an especially exalted understanding of what such freedom consists in. True human freedom is more than the mere indeterminate power of individuals to choose what they wish to do or to own with as little interference from the state or institutional authorities as possible (though there is certainly nothing contemptible in the desire for real personal liberty and immunity from authoritarian forces). It is the realization of one's nature in its own proper good end, one's ability to flourish in the full range of one's humanity—which for the human person entails freely seeking union with God. It is never then the mere "negative liberty" of indeterminate openness to everything. To be fully free is to be joined to that for which one's nature was

originally framed, and for which, in the depths of one's
soul, one ceaselessly longs. The conventions of human
rights cannot achieve this freedom for any of us; but those
conventions can help to assure individuals and communities liberty from an immense variety of destructive and
corrupting forces that too often conspire to thwart the
pursuit of true freedom. The language of human rights is
indispensable in negotiating the principles of civil justice
and peace, but also serves the highest aspirations of human nature by enunciating and defending the inviolable
dignity of every soul.

$63   The chief philosophical principle animating the con-
ventions of human rights theory is the essential priority
of human dignity, freedom, equality, and justice in the social, civil, and legal constitution of any nation. No set of
laws, no realm of privilege or special concern, no national
or international imperative transcends the absolute moral
demand of human rights upon the state and all its institutions. In every sense, then, the language of human rights
accords with the most fundamental tenets that should in-
form any Christian conscience. Intrinsic to every theory of
human rights, moreover, are certain specific legal, civil, social, and international obligations incumbent upon every
government. Among the legal rights that every state must
protect and promote are a number of basic freedoms, such
as freedom of conscience, freedom of thought, freedom of
speech, freedom of the press, and so forth. There are also
more specific legal protections that must be provided: the
right to safety, the right to legal representation under any
circumstances of forensic prosecution or police investiga-
tion, immunity from unwarranted searches, seizures, or

arrests, protection against incarceration without cause or charge, strict evidentiary standards such as the rule of *habeas corpus*, among other things. Then there are those civil rights that must be regarded as the universal and inalienable possessions of all persons: the right to vote for or against those exercising political power, equal access for all persons to political representation, freedom of association, freedom of religion, the right of peaceful assembly and protest, freedom of workers to form unions, freedom from all forms of forced labor (even for those in prison), protection against segregation, prejudicial policies, or hate crimes, freedom from discrimination in housing or employment on any basis, the right to equal police protections for all persons, protection of non-citizens against unequal treatment, laws insuring humane practices of criminal justice and incarceration, the universal abolition of capital punishment, and so forth. As for the social rights that every government should insure, these include the right to free universal health care, equally available to persons of every economic condition, the right to social security pensions and provisions for the elderly sufficient to insure them dignity and comfort in their last years, the right to infant care, and the right to adequate welfare provisions for the indigent and disabled. As for conventions regarding international rights, these must at the very least presume the right of every people to be protected against aggression and spoliation by foreign powers or corporate interests, preservation of a healthy and habitable environment, protection against and vigorous legal prosecution of war crimes, an absolute prohibition on torture, protection against displacement, the right of flight even when this involves crossing national borders, and the universal right of asylum for those displaced as a result of war, oppression, poverty, civil collapse, natural disaster, or persecution. Again, the conventions of human rights theory cannot accomplish or even address everything that the Orthodox Church desires for human beings; by themselves, these conventions cannot conquer selfishness in human hearts or create enduring forms of community; they cannot provide a comprehensive and compelling vision of the common good that answers all the material, moral, and spiritual needs of human nature. The language of human rights is, in many ways, a minimal language. It is also, however, a usefully concise language that can help to shape and secure rules of charity, mercy, and justice that the Church regards as the very least that should be required of every society; and so it is a language that must be unfailingly affirmed and supported by all Christians in the modern world.

§64   A fundamental human right is the protection of the principle of religious freedom in all its aspects— namely, the freedom of conscience, belief, and religion, including, alone and in community, in private and in public, the right to freedom of worship and practice, the right to manifest one's religion, as well as the right of religious communities to religious education and to the full function and exercise of their religious duties, without any form of direct or indirect interference by the state.[55]

In any society, the struggle for religious freedom and for respect for the conscience of every human being provides the most resplendent proof of the power of love over

---

55   Holy and Great Council, Encyclical, §16.

hatred, of unity over division, of compassion over indifference. A society that protects freedom of religion is one
that recognizes that it is only through the preservation
of a sphere of spiritual concern, transcendent even of the
interests of the state, that a people can sustain the moral
foundations of real civil and social unity. Conscience is
the voice of the divine law within each of us; so the suppression of conscience cannot help but make a nation's
written laws unjust and ultimately self-defeating. Even in
lands where one faith enjoys preponderant dominance,
the rights of the majority can be truly secured against the
encroachments of the state or of unconstrained capital or
of other destructive forces only by guaranteeing the religious rights of all minorities. This is why the Ecumenical
Patriarchate tirelessly seeks to promote the right of free
worship and confession for all peoples. For the measure
with which we honor the faith of others is the measure
with which we can expect our own faith to be honored.

§65   During the Lenten fast of 379 AD, St. Gregory of Nyssa
preached a sermon that was perhaps the first recorded at-
tack on slavery *as an institution* in Western history.[56] Before
then, Stoic and Christian writers had protested the mistreatment of slaves, and had (as with Paul's advice to Philemon) advocated treating bonded servants as the spiritual equals of their masters. But no one before had ever
raised serious questions about the moral legitimacy of the
very existence of bonded servitude. Gregory's argument
was, moreover, entirely based upon Christian principles:
the universality of the divine image in all human beings,
the equality of all persons in the body of Christ, the blood

---

56   Gregory of Nyssa, *On Ecclesiastes*, Homily 4. PG 44.664B.

with which Christ purchased all of humanity for himself, the indivisible unity of all persons as brothers and sisters in Christ, and so on. Christianity was born into a world of masters and slaves, one whose economy was everywhere sustained by the sinful principle that one human being could be the property of another. Though the early Church did not pretend it had the power to end bonded servitude in its society, or even succeed in imagining such a possibility, the Christian community at its best did attempt to create a community and even polity of its own in which the difference of masters and slaves was annulled by the equality of all Christians as fellow heirs of the Kingdom, and therefore as kin one to another. In Christ, proclaimed the Apostle Paul, there is *neither slave nor free person, for all* *Galatians 3:28* *are one in Christ.* Thus he also enjoined the Christian Philemon to receive back his truant slave Onesimus no lon- *Philemon 15–16* ger as a slave at all, but rather as a brother. This prompted St. John Chrysostom to observe that "the Church does not accept a difference between master and servant."[57] Needless to say, Christian society did not over the centuries adhere faithfully to this rule, or properly recognize and accept the dissolution of the institution of slavery that it logically implied. And, in time, Christian culture came to accept an evil it should have eschewed from the first. Only in the modern age has it become fully possible for the Christian world to repent without any duplicity for its failure in this regard to live perfectly in accord with the liberating Gospel of Christ, who came to set the captives free and to pay the price of their emancipation. Even so,

---

57   John Chrysostom, *Commentary on the Letter to Philemon*, Homily 1. PG 62.705B.

the modern world has not been fully purged of this evil institution. The Orthodox Church recognizes that a commitment to human rights in today's world still involves a tireless struggle against all the forms of slavery that still exist in the world. These include not only continued practices of bonded servitude in various quarters of the globe, but a number of other practices as well, both criminal and legally tolerated. This is why the Ecumenical Patriarchate has recently focused attention on modern slavery. Countless children, women, and men throughout the world are currently suffering under various forms of human trafficking: forced labor for both children and adults, the sexual exploitation of children, women, and men, forced and early marriage, conscription of child soldiers, exploitation of migrants and refugees, organ trafficking, and so on. Today we see that large caravans of persons forced to leave their homes and countries due to violence, famine, and poverty are vulnerable to the worst imaginable exploitations, including becoming victims of organized criminal enterprises. At the same time, there are parts of the world where coerced labor, child labor, unremunerated labor, and labor under dangerous conditions are not only permitted, but even encouraged, by governments and businesses. And some nations—even some that have thriving economies—do not hesitate to exploit various kinds of forced labor, especially the labor of convicts. Orthodox Christians must join the effort to eradicate modern slavery in all its forms, across the world and for all time. The Church re-affirms, therefore, the assertion contained in the *Declaration of Religious Leaders against Modern Slavery* (2 December 2014), to which it is a signatory, that slavery is "a crime against humanity," and that Orthodox Christians must join together with all who are committed to do all in their power, within their congregations and beyond, to work for the freedom of all those who are enslaved and trafficked so that their future may be restored. On the way to achieving this end, our adversary is not simply modern slavery, but also the spirit that nourishes it: the deification of profit, the pervasive modern ethos of consumerism, and the base impulses of racism, sexism, and egocentrism.

§66   No moral injunction constitutes a more constant theme in scripture, from the earliest days of the Law and the Prophets to the age of the Apostles, than hospitality and protection for strangers in need. *You shall not wrong or oppress the stranger, for you were yourselves strangers in the* Exodus 22:21; cf. 23:9 *land of Egypt. You shall treat the stranger who lives among you as one native-born, and love him as you do yourself; for you were* Leviticus 19:34 *strangers in the land of Egypt. For the Lord your God ... shows no partiality ... He pronounces justice for the fatherless and the widow, and he loves the stranger, giving him bread and clothing;* Deuteronomy 10:17–19 *so you must love the stranger, for you were strangers in the land* Deuteronomy 27:19 *of Egypt. Cursed is he who withholds justice from the alien. The* Psalm 146[145]:9 *Lord watches over the alien. But no stranger has had to live in* Job 31:32 *the street, for I have opened my doors to the traveler. Is not this the fasting I have required? ... to bring into shelter the poor wan-* Isaiah 58:6–7 *derer ...? I will be swift to prosecute ... those who turn the alien* Malachi 3:5 *away, but who do not fear me, says the Lord of hosts. Do not forget to be hospitable to aliens, for thereby some have unknowingly* Hebrews 13:2 *welcomed angels.* Christ, in fact, tells us that our very salvation depends upon the hospitality we extend to strangers: *Then they too will answer, saying, 'Lord, when did we see you ...*

*a stranger . . . and not minister to you?' And he will reply, 'I tell
you truly, insofar as you did not do it to one of the least of these,
you did not do it to me.'* These words must seem especially   *Matthew 25:44–45*
tormenting—and especially challenging—to Christian
conscience today. The twenty-first century dawned as a
century of migrants and refugees fleeing violent crime,
poverty, climate change, war, drought, economic collapse,
and asking for safety, sustenance, and hope. The developed world everywhere knows the presence of refugees
and asylum-seekers, many legally admitted but also many
others without documentation. They confront the consciences of wealthier nations daily with their sheer vul-
nerability, indigence, and suffering. This is a global crisis, but also a personal appeal to our faith, to our deepest
moral natures, to our most inabrogable responsibilities.

§67   The Orthodox Church regards the plight of these displaced peoples as nothing less than a divine call to love,
justice, service, mercy, and inexhaustible generosity. The
Church's absolute obligation to defend the dignity and
take up the cause of migrants, refugees, and asylum-seekers is clearly stated in the Encyclical of the Holy and Great
Council:

> The contemporary and ever-intensifying refugee
> and migrant crisis, due to political, economic and
> environmental causes, is at the center of the world's
> attention. The Orthodox Church has always treated
> and continues to treat those who are persecuted, in
> danger and in need on the basis of the Lord's words:
> *I was hungry and you gave me to eat, I was thirsty and you
> gave me to drink, and was a stranger and you took me in,
> I was naked and you clothed me, I was sick and you vis-
> ited me, in prison and you came to me,* and *Truly I tell you,*   *Matthew 25:35-36*

Matthew 25:40

cf. Matthew 11:28

Ephesians 4:12

whatever you did for one of the least of these my brethren, you did for me. Throughout its history, the Church was always on the side of the *weary and heavy laden.* At no time was the Church's philanthropic work limited merely to circumstantial good deeds toward the needy and suffering, but rather it sought to eradicate the causes that create social problems. The Church's *work of service* is recognized by everyone. We appeal therefore, first of all, to those able to remove the causes for the creation of the refugee crisis to take the necessary positive decisions. We call on the civil authorities, the Orthodox faithful and the other citizens of the countries in which they have sought refuge and continue to seek refuge to accord them every possible assistance, even from out of their own insufficiency.[58]

The Church therefore praises those nations that have received these migrants and refugees, and that have granted asylum to those who seek it. Moreover, it reminds Christians everywhere that such welcome is a biblical command that transcends the interests of secular governments. The modern nation-state is not a sacred institution, even if it can at times serve the causes of justice, equity, and peace. Nor are borders anything more than accidents of history and conventions of law. They too may have at times a useful purpose to serve, but in themselves they are not moral or spiritual goods whose claim upon us can justify failing in our sacred responsibilities to those whom God has commended to our special care. In our own time, we have seen some European governments and a great many ideologues affecting to defend "Christian Europe" by seeking

---

58   Paragraph 19.

completely to seal borders, by promoting nationalist and even racialist ideas, and by rejecting in countless other ways the words of Christ himself. We have seen nativist panic encouraged in Europe, in Australia, in the Americas. In the United States, the most powerful and wealthiest nation in history—one, in fact, born out of mighty floods of immigrants from around the world—we have seen political leaders not only encouraging fear and hatred of asylum-seekers and impoverished immigrants, but even employing terror against them: abducting children from their parents, shattering families, tormenting parents and children alike, interning all of them indefinitely, denying due process to asylum-seekers, slandering and lying about those seeking refuge, deploying the military at southern borders to terrify and threaten unarmed migrants, employing racist and nativist rhetoric against asylum-seekers for the sake of political advantage, and so forth. All such actions are assaults upon the image of God in those who seek our mercy. They are offenses against the Holy Spirit. In the name of Christ, the Orthodox Church denounces these practices, and implores those who are guilty of them to repent and to seek instead to become servants of justice and charity.

VIII. SCIENCE, TECHNOLOGY, AND THE NATURAL WORLD

Your own of your own we offer to you

$68   Ours is an age of ever more rapid technological development; humanity's power today to transform physical reality, for both good and ill, is quite unprecedented in human history, and constitutes both a peril and a

responsibility for which humanity seems largely unpre-
pared. The Orthodox Church must, therefore, before all
else, remind Christians that the world we inhabit is God's
good creation (however marred by sin and death it may
be), and a gracious gift to all his creatures. With St. Maximus the Confessor, it affirms that the human presence
in the physical cosmos is also a spiritual office, a kind
of cosmic priesthood. Humanity occupies the place of a
methorios, the boundary where the spiritual and material
realms meet and are united; and, through that priestly
mediation, the light of spirit pervades all of created nature, while the whole of cosmic existence is raised up into
spiritual life. This is, at least, creation as God intends it,
and as it will exist in the restoration of all things, when
he brings about a renewed heaven and earth where all
the creatures of land, sea, and air will rejoice in his light.
Christians must always recall that, according to the teachings of their faith, the bondage of creation to death is the
consequence of humanity's apostasy from its priestly role;
that in Christ this priesthood has been restored; and that
the ultimate salvation promised in scripture encompass-
es the whole of cosmic reality, and so will be made perfect only in a renewed creation (one that scripture repeatedly portrays as abounding in animal and plant life, no
less than human). The responsibility of Christians in this
world, therefore, in seeking to transfigure fallen nature in
service to the Kingdom, involves a real responsibility to
the whole of creation and a ceaseless concern for its integrity and flourishing. How to accomplish this in an age
of such rapid technological change and of such immense
technological power is a question that Christians must

ceaselessly pose for themselves, and that the Church must approach with prayerful discernment. This is the foundation and context of the pioneering initiatives of the Ecumenical Patriarchate for the preservation of the natural environment. It is also the reason and reasoning behind the establishment of September 1—as early as in 1989, by Ecumenical Patriarch Demetrios, of blessed memory, and subsequently adopted by all Orthodox Churches, by the World Council of Churches and many Protestant Confessions, by the Anglican Communion, as well as by Pope Francis for the Roman Catholic Church—as the annual day of prayer for and protection of God's creation.

§69   The Christian's mission to transfigure the world in the light of God's Kingdom is one that reaches out to all of creation, to all of life, to every dimension of cosmic existence. Wherever there is suffering, Christians are called to bring healing as relief and reconciliation. This is why the Church early in its history began founding hospitals open to all persons, and employing such therapies and medicines as were known in their day. St. Basil's extraordinary Basiliad was a place of welfare for the poor even as it was a place of wholeness for the sick. As St. Basil wrote, "Medicine is a gift from God even if some people do not make the right use of it. Granted, it would be stupid to put all hope of a cure in the hands of doctors, yet there are people who stubbornly refuse their help altogether."[59] The ministry of healing has been recognized by the Church from her earliest days as a holy endeavor and as a genuine cooperation in God's workings. And in no area of human activity is technological development more readily

---

59   Basil, *Longer Rules*, Question 55. PG 31.1048B.

to be sought and welcomed than in the medical sciences. The invention of medicines, antibiotics, vaccines, therapies for even the gravest of illnesses, and so forth, are especially glorious achievements of human creativity, and are thus also particularly precious gifts from God. Even so, the speed with which the medical sciences today develop, test, and use new technologies and therapies often far outpaces moral reflection and spiritual discernment. More and more, the Church must be willing to consider and evaluate every medical innovation separately, as it appears, and sometimes to consider the uses of these innovations on a case-by-case basis. This will often prove necessary, for instance, in the Church's approach to the forms of care given the elderly and the terminally ill. There can be no simple general rule, for example, as to when to continue medical treatment to prolong life and when instead to refrain from doing so. The welfare of the patient, the spiritual and material welfare of his or her family, the sensible distinction between ordinary and extraordinary efforts to preserve and prolong life—all of these issues, as well as many others, must be taken into consideration in each individual case. Often the judgment that the Church will render on current medical technologies depends on the practical and moral concomitants of those technologies, which is to say the methods they require and the ethical consequences those methods might entail. For instance, some practices of *in vitro* fertilization or stem-cell treatments for spinal injuries may involve the destruction of very young human embryos, and this the Church cannot support. Again, each individual case of treatment may need to be adjudicated separately. The Church might, for example, give its full blessing to a particular stem-cell therapy to alleviate symptoms of a particular spinal injury so long as the stem-cells used have not been extracted from aborted babies.

§70   New technologies evolve even more rapidly outside the realm of medical science, it might be argued. Certainly, they do so with greater diversity and cultural pervasiveness. In only the past few years, for instance—scarcely more than a decade or two—we have seen radical new developments in technologies of communication, datagathering and sorting, mass-messaging, instant global proliferation of information (or misinformation, as the case may be), and so forth. Each such development brings with it numerous beneficial possibilities, such as extremely rapid humane interventions in situations of natural catastrophe or human aggression, or such as new avenues of communication and reciprocal understanding between persons or peoples. Yet these same technologies create new opportunities for malicious abuse or inadvertently harmful misuse. Today, the distinctions between reality and fantasy, between facts and opinions, between news and ideologically motivated propaganda, and between truth and lies have become ever more obscure and fluid, precisely as a result of the enormous power of the internet. We have seen numerous cases in recent years of the systematic corruption of public discourse on the internet by agents of confusion, for the purpose of sowing discord or influencing political trends, principally through deceit and misdirection. Just as pernicious, perhaps, are the unplanned but still quite ubiquitous corruptions induced by the precipitous decline of civility on the internet. The casual and customary use of the rhetoric of blame, provocation, and insult, cruelty, harassment, and humiliation—all of these spiritually devastating practices are all too common to the atmosphere of internet culture. It may well be that the very nature of modern instantaneous communication makes such evils all but inevitable. The disembodied, curiously impersonal, and abstracted quality of virtual communication seems to prompt the kind of amoral and self-absorbed behavior that the real, immediate presence of another person would discourage. Here communication can all too often become an alternative to true communion, and in fact destructive of such communion. We know also that the internet can (for many of the same reasons) become a remarkably powerful vehicle for any number of obsessions and addictive fixations, such as pornography or violent fantasy. As yet, it is impossible to predict the extent either of the good or of the harm that the new age of instantaneous global interconnection may bring about. But the magnitude of the latter will almost certainly be no smaller than that of the former, and will in many unforeseen ways be greater. Here the Church must be vigilant regarding the effects of these new technologies and wise in combatting their more deleterious effects. It must also remain constantly aware of even more consequential developments in other or related spheres of research, such as new algorithms for artificial intelligence or new techniques of gene-editing. How well it will be able to marshal its pastoral powers and resources in the face of this ever-accelerating process of scientific advancement will surely determine how well it will be able to offer true spiritual refuge to those who seek God and his love in the modern world.

§71   Perhaps the Church's first concern, in seeking to understand the rapid technological developments of late modernity, and in attempting to secure her role as a place of spiritual stability amid the incessant flux of scientific and social change, should be to strive to overcome any apparent antagonism between the world of faith and that of the sciences. One of the more insidious aspects of modern Western cultural history has been the emergence of religious fundamentalism, including fideistic forms of Christianity that refuse to accept discoveries in such fields as geology, paleontology, evolutionary biology, genetics, and the environmental sciences. No less fideistic, moreover, are forms of ideological "scientism" and metaphysical "materialism" that insist that all of reality is reducible to purely material forces and causes, and that the entire realm of the spiritual is an illusion. Neither scientific evidence nor logic supports such a view of reality; indeed, it is philosophically incoherent. But, even so, the popular intellectual culture of late modernity has been marked to a remarkable degree by these opposed fundamentalisms. The Orthodox Church has no interest in hostilities between simpleminded philosophies, much less in historically illiterate fables regarding some kind of perennial conflict between faith and scientific reason. Christians should rejoice in the advances of all the sciences, gladly learn from them, and promote scientific education, as well as public and private funding for legitimate and necessary scientific research. In our age of ecological crisis especially, we must draw on all the resources of scientific research and theory to seek out an ever deeper knowledge of our world, and ever more effective solutions to our shared dangers. In the eyes of the Church, all that contributes to the welfare of humanity and of creation as a whole is to be praised, and it offers her ceaseless encouragement to researchers in the relevant fields to devote their best efforts to the alleviation of suffering everywhere, including the development of new technologies for providing clean water to deprived regions, preventing soil depletion and crop disease, increasing crop yields and crop durability, and so forth. And the Church encourages the faithful to be grateful for—and to accept—the findings of the sciences, even those that might occasionally oblige them to revise their understandings of the history and frame of cosmic reality. The desire for scientific knowledge flows from the same wellspring as faith's longing to enter ever more deeply into the mystery of God.

§72   Neither should the Church fail to take advantage of the resources of the sciences for her own pastoral ministry, as well as the technological advances of the internet and social media for her pastoral mission. At the very least, her pastoral practices should be informed by what has been learned in recent centuries regarding the complexity of human motivations and desires, and regarding the hidden physical and psychological causes—including genetic, neurobiological, biochemical, and psychologically traumatic causes—that often contribute to human behavior. In no way need this awareness detract from the Church's understanding of the real power of sin in the world or of the necessity in every life for repentance and forgiveness; nor need it encourage the Church to dismiss spiritual maladies as purely psychological disorders, requiring therapies but not genuine penitence and regeneration by

God's Spirit. But a keen sense of the larger predicament of embodied spirits in a world tormented by death and spiritual disorder can only aid Orthodox pastors in understanding, persuading, and healing the souls in their charge. And it is entirely in keeping with true charity and true Christian humility for such pastors to recognize that certain problems are as much the result of purely contingent physical or psychological forces as of moral failings on anyone's part. Those who devote themselves to the care of souls should be willing and even eager to learn from those who study the natural dynamisms of minds and bodies, and to be grateful to God for the grace he supplies through the insights these latter can provide.

$73   In the Church's central symbol and declaration of faith, the Nicene-Constantinopolitan Creed, Orthodox Christians confess "one God, maker of heaven and earth, and of all things visible and invisible." Scripture affirms that *God saw everything that was made and, indeed, it was very good.* *Genesis 1:31* The word for "good" *(kalon)* in the canonical Greek text connotes more than just the value of a thing, and more even than its mere moral acceptability; it indicates that the world was also created as, and was called to be, "beautiful." The Liturgy of St. James affirms this too: "For the one God is Trinity, whose glory the heavens declare, while earth proclaims his dominion, the sea his might and every physical and immaterial creature his greatness." This profound belief in the goodness and beauty of all creation is the source and substance of the Church's whole cosmic vision. As Orthodox Christians sing at the Feast of the Theophany: "The nature of waters is sanctified, the earth is blessed, and the heavens are enlightened" . . . "so that by the elements of creation, and by the angels, and by human beings, by things both visible and invisible, God's most holy name may be glorified" (From the Great Blessing of the Waters). St. Maximus the Confessor tells us that human beings are not isolated from the rest of creation; they are bound, by their very nature, to the whole of creation.[60] And when humankind and creation are thus rightly related, humanity is fulfilling its vocation to bless, elevate, and *transfigure* the cosmos, so that its intrinsic goodness might be revealed even amidst its fallenness. In this, God's most holy name is glorified. Nevertheless, human beings all too often imagine themselves to be something separate and apart from the rest of creation, involved in the material world only insofar as they can or must exploit it for their own ends; they ignore, neglect, and even at times willfully reject their bond to the rest of creation. Again and again, humankind has denied its vocation to transfigure the cosmos, and has instead disfigured our world. And ever since the birth of the industrial age, humanity's capacity for harm has been relentlessly magnified. As a result, we today find ourselves faced with such previously unimaginable catastrophes as the increased melting of ice-caps and glaciers, rain and rivers running sour from pollution, pharmaceuticals tainting our drinking-water, and the tragic reduction or even extinction of many species. Over against all the forces—political, social, and economic, corporate and civic, spiritual and material—that contribute to the degradation of our ecosystems, the Church seeks to cultivate a truly liturgical and sacramental path

60   Maximus, *Mystagogia* 7 PG 91.684, in *Maximus Confessor: Select writings*, New York, NY: Paulist Press, 1985, 196.

to communion with God in and through his creation, one that necessarily demands compassion for all others and care for all of creation.

§74   The work of cosmic transfiguration requires great effort, a ceaseless striving against the fallen aspects of humanity and of the world; and the embrace of this labor requires an ascetic ethos, one that can reorient the human will in such a way as to restore its bond with all of creation. Such an ethos reminds Christians that creation, as a divine gift from the loving creator, exists not simply as ours to consume at whim or will, but rather as a realm of communion and delight, in whose goodness all persons and all creatures are meant to share, and whose beauty all persons are called to cherish and protect. Among other things, this entails working to eliminate wasteful and destructive uses of natural resources, working to preserve the natural world for the present generation and for all generations to come, and practicing restraint and wise frugality in all things. None of this, however, is likely possible without a deep training in gratitude. Without thanksgiving, we are not truly human. This, in fact, is the very foundation of the Church's Eucharistic understanding of itself and of its mission in the world. When humanity is in harmony with all of creation, this thanksgiving comes effortlessly and naturally. When that harmony is ruptured or replaced by discord, as it so often is, thanksgiving becomes instead an obligation to be discharged, sometimes with difficulty; but only such thanksgiving can truly heal the division that alienates humanity from the rest of the created order. When human beings learn to appreciate the earth's resources in a truly eucharistic spirit, they can no longer treat creation as something separate from themselves, as mere utility or property. Then they become able truly to offer the world back up to its creator in genuine thanksgiving—"Your own of your own we offer to you, in all and for all" (From the Anaphora in the Divine Liturgy of St. John Chrysostom)—and in that act of worship creation is restored to itself: everything assumes again its purpose, as intended by God from the beginning, and is to some degree arrayed again in its primordial beauty.

§75   The Church understands that this world, as God's creation, is a sacred mystery whose depths reach down into the eternal counsels of its maker; and this in and of itself precludes any of the arrogance of mastery on the part of human beings. Indeed, exploitation of the world's resources should always be recognized as an expression of Adam's "original sin" rather than as a proper way of receiving God's wonderful gift in creation. Such exploitation is the result of selfishness and greed, which arise from humanity's alienation from God, and from humanity's consequent loss of a rightly ordered relationship with the rest of nature. Thus, as we have repeatedly stressed, every act of exploitation, pollution, and misuse of God's creation must be recognized as sin. The Apostle Paul describes creation as *groaning in pain along with us from the beginning till now*, while *awaiting with eager longing* for *glorious liberation by the children of God*. The effects of sin and of our alienation from God are not only personal and social, but also ecological and even cosmic. Hence, our ecological crisis must be seen not merely as an ethical dilemma; it is an ontological and theological issue that demands a radical

Romans 8:22
Romans 8:19
Romans 8:21

change of mind and a new way of being. And this must entail altering our habits not only as individuals, but as a species. For instance, our often heedless consumption of natural resources and our wanton use of fossil fuels have induced increasingly catastrophic processes of climate change and global warming. Therefore, our pursuit of alternative sources of energy and our efforts to reduce our impact on the planet as much as possible are now necessary expressions of our vocation to transfigure the world.

§76   None of us exists in isolation from the whole of humanity, or from the totality of creation. We are dependent creatures, creatures ever in communion, and hence we are also morally responsible not only for ourselves or for those whom we immediately influence or affect, but for the whole of the created order—the whole city of the cosmos, so to speak. In our own time, especially, we must understand that serving our neighbor and preserving the natural environment are intimately and inseparably connected. There is a close and indissoluble bond between our care of creation and our service to the body of Christ, just as there is between the economic conditions of the poor and the ecological conditions of the planet. Scientists tell us that those most egregiously harmed by the current ecological crisis will continue to be those who have the least. This means that the issue of climate change is also an issue of social welfare and social justice. The Church calls, therefore, upon the governments of the world to seek ways of advancing the environmental sciences, through education and state subventions for research, and to be willing to fund technologies that might serve to reverse the dire effects of carbon emissions, pollution, and all forms of environmental degradation.

$77   We must also recall, moreover, that human beings are part of the intricate and delicate web of creation, and that their welfare cannot be isolated from the welfare of the whole natural world. As St. Maximus the Confessor argued, in Christ all the dimensions of humanity's alienation from its proper nature are overcome, including its alienation from the rest of the physical cosmos; and Christ came in part to restore to material creation its original nature as God's earthly paradise.[61] Our reconciliation with God, therefore, must necessarily express itself also in our reconciliation with nature, including our reconciliation with animals. It is no coincidence that the creation narrative of Genesis describes the making of animal life and *Genesis 1:24–31* the making of humanity as occurring on the same day. Nor should it be forgotten that, according to the story of the Great Flood, Noah's covenant with God encompasses the animals in the ark and all their descendants, in perpe- *Genesis 9:9–11* tuity. The unique grandeur of humanity in this world, the image of God within each person, is also a unique responsibility and ministry, a priesthood in service to the whole of creation in its anxious longing for God's glory. Humanity shares the earth with all other living things, but singularly among living creatures possesses the ability and authority to care for it (or, sadly, to destroy it). The animals that fill the world are testament to the bounty of God's creative love, its variety and richness; and all the beasts of the natural order are enfolded in God's love; not even a single

---

61   Maximus, *Ambiguum* 41. PG 91.1305CD. See *On Difficulties in the Church Fathers*, vol. 2, 103–121.

sparrow falls without God seeing. Moreover, animals by   *Matthew 10:29*
their very innocence remind us of the paradise that hu-
man sin has squandered, and their capacity for blameless
suffering reminds us of the cosmic cataclysm induced by
humanity's alienation from God. We must recall also that
all the promises of scripture regarding the age that is to
come concern not merely the spiritual destiny of humanity, but the future of a redeemed cosmos, in which plant
and animal life are plentifully present, renewed in a condition of cosmic harmony.

§78   Thus, in the lives of the saints, there are numerous sto-
ries about wild beasts, of the kind that would normally
be horrifying or hostile to human beings, drawn to the
kindness of holy men and women. In the seventh century,
Abba Isaac of Nineveh defined a merciful heart as "a heart
burning for the sake of the entire creation, for people, for
birds, for animals ... and for every created thing."[62] This is
a consistent theme in the witness of the saints. St. Gera-
simos healed a wounded lion near the Jordan River; St.
Hubertus, having received a vision of Christ while hunt-
ing deer, proclaimed an ethic of conservation for hunters;
St. Columbanus befriended wolves, bears, birds, and rabbits; St. Sergius tamed a wild bear; St. Seraphim of Sarov
fed the wild animals; St. Mary of Egypt may well have befriended the lion that guarded her remains; St. Innocent
healed a wounded eagle; St. Melangell was known for her
protection of wild rabbits and the taming of their preda-
tors; in the modern period, St. Paisios lived in harmony
with snakes. And not only animals, but plants as well, must

---

62   Abba Isaac the Syrian, *Ascetic Treatises* [In Greek] 62, Holy Monastery of
Iveron: Mount Athos, 2012, 736.

be objects of our love. St. Kosmas the Aetolian preached that "people will remain poor, because they have no love for trees"[63] and St. Amphilochios of Patmos asked, "Do you know that God gave us one more commandment that is not recorded in scripture? It is the commandment to love the trees." The ascetic ethos and the eucharistic spirit of the Orthodox Church perfectly coincide in this great sacramental vision of creation, which discerns the traces of God's presence "everywhere present and filling all things" (Prayer to the Holy Spirit) even in a world still as yet languishing in bondage to sin and death. It is a vision, moreover, that perceives human beings as bound to all of creation, as well as one that encourages them to rejoice in the goodness and beauty of the whole world. This ethos and this spirit together remind us that gratitude and wonder, hope and joy, are our only appropriate—indeed, our truly creative and fruitful—attitude in the face of the ecological crisis now confronting the planet, because they alone can give us the willingness and the resolve to serve the good of creation as unremittingly as we must, out of love for it and its creator.

IX. CONCLUSION

Let us the faithful rejoice, having this anchor of hope[64]

§79 Needless to say, a document of this sort can address only so many issues and its authors can foresee only so many of the additional concerns that might occur to those who receive it. It is offered, therefore, with the caution and the

---

63   *Prophecy* 96.

64   From the Canon on the Feast of Pascha.

humble acknowledgment that it is in many respects quite inadequate as a comprehensive statement of the social ethos of the Church. In that sense, it is at most an invitation to further and deeper reflection on the parts of the faithful. More to the point, the social ethos of the Church is fulfilled not simply through the implementation of ethical prescriptions, but also and most fully in the liturgical expectation of the divine Kingdom. Nothing written here can bear much fruit if taken in abstraction from the full sacramental life of those who are called to be immersed in the fire of the Holy Spirit, joined thereby to Christ and, through Christ, to the Father. For the Church Fathers, and especially in the teaching of Dionysius the Areopagite, the heavenly doxology of the angelic powers and righteous orders surrounding the royal throne of Christ at once per- *cf. Revelation 7:11* fects and communicates the archetypal and consummate worship to which all creation is summoned from everlasting, and it is this heavenly liturgy that inspires and informs the earthly, Eucharistic sacrament.[65] This indissoluble and inalienable relationship between the heavenly polity of the angelic powers and saints and the earthly life of the Church in the world provides the essential rationale underlying the ethical principles of the Gospel and the Church; for those principles are nothing less than a way of participation in the eternal ecstasy of worship that is alone able to fulfill created natures and elevate them to their divine destiny. For Orthodox Christians to conform themselves to Christ's moral commandments, however, each must also take up his or her personal cross daily, and

---

65   See *Pseudo-Dionysius: The Complete Works*, ed. Colin Luibheid, Mahwah, NJ: Paulist Press, 1987.

this must in some measure involve the ascetical discipline of "joyful mourning"—not as some sort of cathartic discharge of emotion, but rather as an act of repentance for one's alienation from the grace of God. This is why, in the Beatitudes, those who mourn are blessed by Christ, who pledges the certainty of divine consolation. *Blessed are* *those who mourn; for they shall be comforted.*

Matthew 5:4

$80
John 17:11, 14–15

   The Church exists *in the world*, but is *not of the world.* It inhabits this life on the threshold between earth and heaven, and bears witness from age to age of things as yet not seen. The Church dwells among the nations as a sign and image of the permanent and perpetual peace of God's Kingdom, and as a promise of the complete healing of humanity and the restoration of a created order shattered by sin and death. Those who are *in Christ* are already *a new* *creation: the old has passed away, behold, the new has come.* This is the glory of the Kingdom of the Father, Son, and Holy Spirit, which even now can be glimpsed in the radiant and transfigured faces of the saints. Yet the Church is not only the living icon of the Kingdom, but is also a ceaseless prophetic witness of hope and joy in a world wounded by its rejection of God. This prophetic vocation demands a refusal to remain silent in the face of injustices, falsehoods, cruelties, and spiritual disorders; and this is not always easy, even in modern free societies. Characteristic of many of our contemporary societies, and curiously common to their otherwise often incompatible political systems in both East and West, is the novel teaching that there is such a thing as a purely public sphere that, in order to be at once both neutral and universal, must exclude religious expression. Religion, moreover, is understood

2 Corinthians 5:17

in such societies as essentially a private pursuit, which must not intrude upon public discussions of the common good. But this is false in principle and, almost invariably, oppressive in practice. For one thing, secularism itself is a form of modern ideology, invested with its own implicit concept of the good and the just; and, if it is imposed too imperiously upon a truly diverse society, it becomes just another authoritarian creed. In some contemporary societies, religious voices in public spaces have been legally and forcibly silenced, whether by the prohibition of religious symbols or even certain religious styles of dress, or by the denial that religious persons can act according to their consciences on matters of ethical import without violating the inalienable rights of others. In truth, human beings cannot erect impermeable partitions between their moral convictions and their deepest beliefs about the nature of reality, and to ask or force them to do so is an invitation to resentment, deepening factionalism, fundamentalism, and strife. It is undeniably the case that modern societies are increasingly culturally diverse; and, far from lamenting this fact, the Orthodox Church celebrates every opportunity for encounter and reciprocal understanding between persons and peoples. But such understanding becomes impossible if certain voices are proleptically silenced by coercive law; and, in the absence of that understanding, and perhaps partly as a result of that coercion, problems far worse and far more destructive than mere civil disagreement can incubate and grow beyond the margins of the sanitized public arena. The Orthodox Church, therefore, cannot accept the relegation of religious conscience and conviction to some purely private sphere, if for no other reason than that her faith in God's Kingdom necessarily shapes every aspect of life for the faithful, including their views on political, social, and civil issues. Neither can the Church simply grant the obvious congeniality, disinterestedness, and impartiality of secularism in the abstract; every ideology can become oppressive when it is given unchallenged power to dictate the terms of public life. While a modest secular order that does not impose a religion on its citizens is a perfectly good and honorable ideal, a government that restricts even ordinary expressions of religious identity and belief all too easily becomes a soft tyranny that will, in the end, create more division than unity.

§81   That said, the Church respects and even reveres the essential freedom of every person, implanted in him or her from the beginning by virtue of the indwelling divine image. This freedom must include both the liberty to accept and love God as revealed in Jesus Christ as well as the liberty to reject the Christian Gospel and embrace other beliefs. Hence, the Church is called at all times and in all places to witness, at one and the same time, both to a vision of the human person as transfigured by fidelity to the will of the Father, as revealed in Jesus Christ, and also to the inviolability of the real freedom of every human person, including the freedom to reject that fidelity. Once again, the Church affirms the goodness of social and political diversity, and asks only that it be a genuine diversity, one that allows for true freedom of conscience and the free expression of belief. Its own mission is to proclaim Christ and him crucified to all peoples and at all times, and to summon everyone into the life of God's Kingdom.

And this mission necessarily includes a sustained dialogue with contemporary culture, and the clear enunciation of a truly Christian vision of social justice and political equity in the midst of the modern world.

§82   *God did not send his Son into the world to judge the world, but that, through him, the world might be saved.* The Orthodox Church sees it as its calling to condemn cruelty and injustice, the economic and political structures that abet and preserve poverty and inequality, the ideological forces that encourage hatred and bigotry; but it is not its calling to condemn the world, or nations, or souls. The Church's mission is to manifest the saving love of God given in Jesus Christ to all creation: a love broken and seemingly defeated upon the cross, but shining out in triumph from the empty tomb at Pascha; a love that imparts eternal life to a world darkened and disfigured by sin and death; a love often rejected, and yet longed for unceasingly, in every heart. It speaks to all persons and every society, calling them to the sacred work of transfiguring the world in the light of God's Kingdom of love and eternal peace. All this being so, this commission humbly offers this document to all who are disposed to listen to its counsels, and especially encourages all the Orthodox faithful—clergy and laity, women and men—to engage in prayerful discussion of this statement, to promote the peace and justice it proclaims, and to seek ways in which to contribute in their own local parishes and communities to the work of the Kingdom. To this end, the revitalization of the order of the diaconate, male and female, may serve as an instructive way of assimilating and applying the principles and guidelines proposed in this statement. The commission

John 3:17

also asks Orthodox seminaries, universities, monasteries, parishes, and associated organizations to foster reflection upon this document, to excuse its deficiencies, to attempt to dilate upon its virtues, and to facilitate its reception by the faithful. It is the earnest prayer of all who have been associated with this document that what is written here will help to advance the work inaugurated in 2016 by the Holy and Great Council of the Orthodox Church, and will further aid in fulfilling the will of God in his Church and in the world.

INDEX